Delighting your customers ... on a Shoestring

Delivering excellent customer service without breaking the bank

Avril Owton MBE

BLOOMSBURY

First published in Great Britain 2007 by A & C Black Publishers Ltd

This edition published 2011 by

Bloomsbury Publishing Plc
50 Bedford Square, London WC1B 3DP

www.acblack.com

A CIP record for this book is available from the British Library.

ISBN: 9-781-4081-3992-9

This book is produced using paper that is made from wood grown in managed, sustainable forests. It is natural, renewable and recyclable. The logging and manufacturing processes conform to the environmental regulations of the country of origin.

Design by Fiona Pike, Pike Design, Winchester
Typeset by RefineCatch Limited, Bungay, Suffolk
Printed and bound by CPI Group (UK) Ltd, Croydon, CR0 4YY

For my late husband, Tom

CONTENTS

ACKNOWLEDGEMENTS

Many people have helped me write this book, but I would particularly like to thank my children, Amanda, Graeme, Emma and Helen, who have all encouraged me to keep going and to not give up! My thanks also to: my dear friend David; Maxine Benson and Karen Gill of Everywoman Ltd; Angela Baker; Larry Hirst; Karl Jones of KNdesign; David Henley; and Lisa Carden of Bloomsbury whose support, guidance and patience have given me the opportunity to achieve one of my ambitions.

INTRODUCTION

About this book

Abraham Lincoln once famously said that 'a woman's skirt should be long enough to cover the subject, but short enough to be interesting'. That is what this book sets out to do: it gets to grips with all the key ways to delight your customers, even if you're on a tight budget. It offers advice that really works and that will have a positive impact on your business, whatever its size and whatever the industry.

It's not just smaller companies that need to pay attention to the quality of customer service they provide. In fact, it's often the larger, well-known high street names that are the weakest in providing good customer care, even though they have the largest training budgets at their disposal. For the smaller business, this can only be encouraging news because you don't need to spend a fortune to build strong and profitable relationships with your customers.

About me

I own and run the award-winning Cloud Hotel in the New Forest. Although I have worked in the service industry for 35 years, I originally trained as a ballet dancer, and I believe the training I had as a dancer gave me the stamina, discipline, drive and perseverance I've needed in business. To me, running your own business is just another performance and the parallels are endless. In order to make your business profitable and keep your customers happy, you've got to be committed, energetic, imaginative, enthusiastic and passionate about your business. You need to keep ahead of the game, too, or someone will step in, get ahead and win the business from you.

In the early 1960s I joined the Tiller Girls dance troupe and we appeared every week on the popular television programme *Sunday Night at the London Palladium*. We worked as a team and were expected to delight our audience — our customers — at every performance. The applause was our reward; we were delighted that we had given so much pleasure to so many people. It was a win-win situation: the audience went away happy and we were happy. We worked hard to perfect our routines: we certainly knew pain and we smiled through it all. It was to be a great training for my future business career.

In 1974 I married a hotelier. The service industry was a new experience for me but, like the theatre, it involved long, unsociable hours and my training as a dancer has certainly helped me to survive. In 1991 I was widowed and had to take over the running of the hotel. I didn't know a bottom line from a chorus line and had a vast amount to learn, but I've found that delighting your customers, and controlling your costs as part of that process, with an effective team of people, is the key to developing a successful and profitable business.

In 2008 I was appointed MBE for service to hospitality and my charity work in Hampshire.

Working in the service industry is probably the best way to develop customer-related skills, but don't worry if you haven't had much experience in this sector. This book extends far beyond the hotel and restaurant business and takes you through the process step by step. It also includes plenty of examples from other industries, where we can see the basics of good customer service used well.

The first thing to remember is that, whatever the nature of your business, your customers are your driving force. They pay the wages (including your own) and it's essential to take them seriously and cater to *their* needs, not yours. We are all customers every single day, whether we're out shopping, visiting the dentist, staying in a hotel, having dinner at a restaurant, being a spectator at a sports event or visiting the theatre. For a business to be successful and profitable, it must have happy customers who want to return and use its services and products again and again. These days customers are looking for more than a good product and great service, they are also looking for an experience that is unique and that they remember. If you give customers an enjoyable experience when they use your services, they'll hopefully tell other people about it, and you will gain more customers. Always give your best and a little bit more because good customer service can take your business from good to great.

It sounds straightforward doesn't it? So why is it that we all want to be treated well as a customer and enjoy the experience, but sometimes find it difficult to make a customer happy when we're on the other side of the desk or the other end of the phone? There are many potential reasons for this, but I think it is our attitude to service that needs to change. Read on to find out how you can provide your customers with an unforgettable experience so they become loyal customers.

1 UNDERSTANDING YOUR CUSTOMERS

If happy customers are the key to a successful business, you have to be able to understand them and know what they want in order to delight them. It's only then that you can begin to anticipate and satisfy their needs and expectations, and give them what they're looking for . . . and a little bit more.

Identifying and targeting your market is crucial: no business could appeal to absolutely everyone, so don't waste your time and precious resources trying. It's impossible to be all things to all people in any area of life, but you can get a head start in business by delivering what people want. The management guru Peter Drucker summed it up perfectly: 'One of the most important things an organisation can do is to determine what business it is in.'

Mind reading

Do *you* know what business you are in? I know I'm in the hospitality industry and offer guests a comfortable place to relax unwind, have a delicious meal and a good night's sleep. Maybe you're a painter and decorator who brings colour to other people's homes, or a project manager who makes sense of other people's lives. How would you describe your business? What would be your strapline?

Looking at the benefits that your products or services offer is crucial. You've probably heard of the 'elevator pitch', a short (less than 30 seconds) statement that enables you to get across what you do in the time it takes you to travel a few floors in a lift with someone. It sounds deceptively easy, but summarising *what* you do and *why* takes some doing. It's worth having a go, however, as it can inform the way in which you work and develop your business: focusing on your core business is the quickest way to keep your customers happy and to grow your business successfully.

For example, how about:

- **We offer a great range of sandwiches and salads, made with the freshest organic ingredients, to office workers in central Liverpool so that they can eat healthily while they're on the go.**
- **My company offers a nationwide widget repair service that reduces downtime, helping contractors to meet their budgets and deadlines.**

In order to truly understand your customers you need to understand what they want and what they need so they become loyal customers. You need to perform the combined functions of psychologist, performer and mind reader. It's hard enough sometimes to understand your close friends and family, let alone customers who start off as strangers. We are all different, not only in our personalities and our expectations of a service, but in our likes and dislikes as well.

One of the best ways of finding out how to please your customers is for you to experience the company, the product and services as a customer yourself, and to then ask yourself a few simple questions:

- How do I feel about the experience I've had?
- What would I want to be changed?
- What did I enjoy?
- If there was a problem, how was it handled?

Of course, this isn't always easy if the business is very small, as your staff would probably recognise your voice if you rang them to place a 'test' order, but you could try e-mailing them from a different account or, if all else fails, ask a family member or friend to help you out. Alternatively, you could employ a 'secret shopper' but they cost money and your budget might not be able to afford one.

When you own or manage a small business, you get many opportunities to have contact with your customers and to get to know them, so take advantage of that. You don't need to do anything elaborate or scary, just engage them in conversation. Start off with a few normal pleasantries, before moving on to some simple but useful questions that will help you build a fuller picture of that person's needs. It's not so necessary to do this for customers who you know well – you must be doing something right if they keep coming back – although it's a good idea to also try and find out what their buying patterns will be in the future so you can be prepared and plan for the growth of your company and retain their loyalty. Customer's preferences can change with time and you don't want to be caught out. It's also very important to build a rapport with relatively new or first-time customers so you get to know them, and their requirements, and hope they become regular customers too. For example, if you run a hotel, you could ask:

- Have you stayed in this area before? If not, let me know if you want any ideas for trips out.

- Have you come here to go walking/ sailing/ climbing (if your area is popular for those activities)?
- Do you have any food allergies, as many people do these days?

If you run a retail business, you could try:

- What have you bought today?
- Have you purchased that make/ model before?
- What type of business are you in (if you're a business-to-business supplier)?
- How often do you tend to replace your equipment?

At its most basic level, customer service is about communicating effectively with your fellow human beings. Getting into the habit of asking these questions will help you to learn more about what your customers want, not only now but also in the future, and how they like to be treated.

That said, it is always a challenge to keep customers happy, because some people are just very difficult to understand. At The Cloud Hotel we sometimes have guests who never smile and who look permanently grumpy and miserable throughout their stay. It doesn't matter how much we try to communicate with them or discover how we can please them, they are relentlessly dour. At the end of their stay, though, the very same people will often tell us how much they have enjoyed their holiday, that they couldn't find anything to complain about, and end up by writing 'excellent stay, we will be back' in our visitors' book.

It is difficult to understand customers like that, although one needs to be aware that they may have a personal or health problem which is making them sad and reserved, but as long as you hear the words 'we'll be back', you know that you have satisfied them. Don't waste valuable time trying to psychoanalyse them!

Do your homework

As we now live in a multicultural society and with many world events being held in the UK such as the Olympic and Paralympic Games, the Ryder Cup and many others it is important to be able to communicate with customers and colleagues from other cultures so we can provide our visitors with five star customer service and understand them.

The amazing array of business information available online is a great help in finding a way of improving customer care. Doing some Internet research doesn't take long and can be fun as well as interesting. One of the many things I discovered while writing this book is that the Japanese do not like the numbers 4 or 9 because of their pronunciation. Four is pronounced 'shi', which is the same pronunciation as 'death,' and nine is pronounced 'ku', which is the same pronunciation as 'agony' or 'torture'. There are hospitals in Japan that don't have these numbers as the room or even the floor number.

This may seem a minor point, but it can help me avert a potentially difficult situation. For instance if I'd booked Japanese customers into room four, and they had asked to be moved to another room but no others were free, I would have had to find another hotel for the customers. Not only would I have lost a customer to a competitor, but it would have created a very uncomfortable atmosphere. So it's crucial that you research your market in order to be able to understand your customers' needs and to respect their individual backgrounds and beliefs. It is to your advantage to take time to learn about the values and expectations of customers from all cultures. A few simple tips can help to make non-English speaking customers feel more welcome.

- Speak slowly and clearly using simple words that they can understand.
- Use appropriate gestures to try to convey what you are trying to say.
- Always smile: a smile means the same in any language and not only makes you feel better but everyone around you.
- Show you have a sense of humour and be patient.

There are 10 million people who are classified as having a disability in the UK and it is important that we attend to, and understand, their needs to be able to give them excellent customer service. The way they are treated and the facilities you provide for them will make them decide if they will give you their business again so it is essential that you train your staff on how to engage with them. Here are a few tips that can help you to accommodate them and to ensure the disabled customers enjoy your product or service.

- Always welcome them and speak directly to the disabled person and not to the person they are with. Just because they are disabled doesn't mean they can't speak for themselves. They hate being patronised.
- Ask what you can do to help them but don't insist. Often they prefer to do things themselves and to be independent.
- Provide them with a ramp if necessary and strong handles for them to grab hold of on steps or slopes.
- If possible, lower a section or your counter for customers in wheelchairs.

■ Remember the partially sighted and provide them with information in large print. For example, if you run a restaurant provide them with a menu with large print and try to seat them at a table with plenty of light.

It's simple really: treat them as you would like to be treated.

These small details can make a difference between customers using your products or service just the once or becoming regulars. You need to inspire your staff to be open minded and have respect for all your customers and to be able to respond to customers of all races, cultures and disabilities. If you provide consistently good service and ensure that these customers are looked after well, they'll keep coming back. And you can do this on a shoestring! The costs are minimal, but the benefits to the business (by way of increased profits) are potentially very large. All it requires is patience and being alert and sensitive to your customers' needs.

All customers, regardless of how much they spend, should receive the same excellent service and any necessary advice or information about your services or products. You want your customers to feel that they have had value for money, as well as an experience that they will remember. Remember, they don't owe you anything; it's up to you to provide them with an experience that will keep them coming back!

Make sure that all your staff have been briefed about your customers and that they can respond positively to a range of unexpected demands and circumstances. It's often the case that friendly personal service and attention to detail will win you more business and loyalty from your customers than investment in new products and new technology. As Canadian restaurateur Mary Kelekis says: 'It's not just running a restaurant; it's being friends with your customers. It's a personal connection.' What better way is there to get to know your customers?

For example, some restaurants and hotels believe it is fashionable to serve food that is decorative but not always plentiful. The result is that many diners go home feeling hungry and perhaps end up having some toast or other snack to satisfy their appetite. Some chefs seem to be trying to be entertainers rather than good cooks. I think all of the television programmes presenting chefs as entertainers rather than cooks must take some responsibility for this attitude. I've been given menus that are almost impossible to understand (and I'm in the industry) and invariably have had to ask the waiter to explain the individual dishes. I've often felt that chefs were cooking for their own enjoyment, rather than the customer's pleasure.

At The Cloud, we've never strayed from serving traditional English food, because that's what our customers expect and enjoy and they are the people we need to please. No, we don't have a Michelin star, but the restaurant is fully booked most days for lunch and is much busier than many of the more sophisticated establishments in the area. Why do you think this is?

Well, it's because I understand my customers. I recognise that there is a high percentage of senior citizens in the area who have the time to go out for lunch, who are looking for comfortable, friendly surroundings and value for money. They are used to traditional fare that satisfies them! I've also found that older clients do not like to be kept waiting for long periods of time and the speed of service can be much quicker when presenting a traditional meal than an elaborately designed picture on a plate.

I benefit from what I call 'the silver £'. With people living longer these days, there are more senior citizens now than ever. In many cases, they have a lot of spending power: their children have grown up, their mortgages are paid off and they have the time to enjoy life. It is potentially a very lucrative market if you can tap into it.

Your core market will, of course, also depend very much on the location and nature of your business, so do consider that carefully when you are working out which customers to target. The Cloud doesn't cater *just* for senior citizens — there's a sizeable market for all ages in any business — but we find that younger customers are generally working or looking after their family during the week, and so tend to come for lunch or dinner at weekends. The chefs have been trained to bear this in mind when creating the daily menus.

There are many facets to running a hotel as there are in any business, be it hospitality, retail, the service industry or recreation to name a few, and I have only reflected on the restaurant trade here, but paying attention to every aspect of your business, and also being responsible for your customers safety and security, will have a very positive impact on the quality of service you give to your customers.

As Paul Gratton, former chief executive of the Internet bank, Egg, says: 'Whatever the business model, it doesn't matter what anybody else thinks if customers don't like it.' That's why it is vital to understand your customers' spending power and know your market. There is no point in setting up a bijou boutique that stocks expensive items in a low-income area, just as there is little sense in a small two-star hotel including very expensive champagne and wines on its wine list. So, while you should offer a good variety of products, they must be within the spending power of your customers. So many small businesses waste money on unnecessary items that their customers are highly unlikely to buy.

Many people are happy with low-key but good-quality services and products; formality can make them feel uncomfortable. For example, a friend of mine once stayed in one of the most luxurious hotels in the world during a business trip.

The hotel's systems were so technically advanced that even trying to work out how to turn on the lights and draw the curtains baffled her. After two days, she felt so stressed at having to work out how to operate everything that when the phone in her room rang, she picked up the hairdryer!

A great deal of money is spent unnecessarily in some businesses. My friend paid a lot to stay at the hotel in question, but she would have had a much more enjoyable stay if she'd been made to feel comfortable and relaxed. As a result of her experience, I decided to stick to conventional light switches, curtains that can be drawn easily, and a real key with which to open the door. Despite the enormous advances in technology over the past few years, many people are still content with the simpler things in life that they can understand and which make them feel at ease. So don't feel threatened by the 'big boys', but use your uniqueness to your advantage by playing to your strengths and their weaknesses. Benjamin Franklin called wasted strengths "Sundials in the shade".

Benefiting from loyalty

You are far more likely to retain customers if they are not made to feel embarrassed or uncomfortable. For instance, single people can feel on edge and vulnerable in certain situations. Being a single person myself, I can empathise, and always try to put single people at ease when they stay at The Cloud overnight or visit our Encore Restaurant for a meal. Even though an increasing number of people live on their own, society is still programmed towards couples. Do bear in mind how many of your customers are likely to be single and don't overlook them, particularly if you are in the hotel or restaurant business. Single people also have friends and family whom they will talk to about their experience of your business and you want to make sure they will give them positive feedback.

As single people often have a disposable income and good spending power, you shouldn't ignore this segment of your market.

Often they end up being seated in the corner of the restaurant or being given a small, dismal room in the hotel. Well, if you think about it, the opposite should happen. A single person has no one to talk to, so they'll enjoy themselves more if they at least have pleasant surroundings and they have often had to pay a huge supplement for their room. At The Cloud we always try to give unaccompanied guests a table with a view, take their order promptly and make them feel very welcome. I have the advantage of knowing how my single customers feel, and it is the responsibility of every business to understand customers' feelings. This way, you will ultimately gain their loyalty.

Loyal customers add significant benefits to the bottom line. Even if a customer spends only £25 a week with you, that adds up to £1,300 over a year. That doesn't even take into account their friends and relatives whom they may influence to become new customers. It's almost impossible to measure the true benefit that a loyal customer brings to the business, but that loyalty does still translate into profit. It costs a business five times less to keep an existing customer than it does to go out and find a new one.

Go that extra mile for your customers and you will find there's less competition. But remember each time you go that extra mile and give a customer a little bit more than they expected, the next time they give you their custom they will expect to receive the same service and so it becomes the norm. Make sure, therefore, that when you do give a customer 'that little bit more', the business can afford it. Here are a few tips to help you provide what others want.

- Treat your customers as you'd want to be treated yourself.
- Talk to them! Passing the time of day with customers and visitors, asking them questions and picking up on

their perceptions of your business is a great way to tune into what they like and what you need to work on.

- Use your friends and family as sounding boards. What is most likely to encourage them to purchase a specific product or service? What techniques or offers do they respond to positively?
- Be visible. There is no better way to get to know your customers than being 'on the shop floor' and interacting with them. I regularly shop at a local small boutique. The owner knows my taste in clothes and always calls me when she has something new in stock that she thinks might appeal to me. She is careful not to harass me and only calls when she is almost certain I will like the new stock. I am always delighted with this personal attention because it saves me so much time and energy. The boutique gets more business, as I've become a loyal customer and have also recommended it to friends. The owner is also astute enough to recognise that I am a walking advertisement for her. She realises that she is in the business of selling and that selling is everything. In a small business you are not only selling a product or service, but you're selling your 'personal brand' too.
- Whenever possible, keep a record of your customers. You don't only want their name, address and telephone number but any other relevant information you can make a note of that may help you discover what they like and (hopefully) initiate another sale in the future. This information helps you to stay close to the customer. If you have sold them a new product, call

them and see if they are happy with their purchase. If they're not, do what you can to rectify the situation.

- Gather feedback in different ways. Some people will happily chat to you about their experiences of your business, but others may find it very difficult to express their views face-to-face. Try to break down the formality so that customers feel relaxed and are able to tell you what they really expect rather than letting them put a negative comment on Facebook or, if you are in hospitality, Tripadvisor. Instead of asking a closed ended question like 'I hope you enjoyed your stay?' You may get a better response if you say 'Is there anything else we could have done to improve your stay?'. Alternatively, offer comment cards or questionnaires that people can complete out at their leisure and give you feedback on your product, service and staff.

- Train your staff how to communicate with, understand and delight your customers. Make sure they realise very clearly that if customers aren't happy with the service they receive, they'll go elsewhere. It only takes one bad experience from a member of staff for you to lose a customer plus all the other people they tell about you and your business. You will never know how much damage that one bad experience has cost you as it can't be measured in numbers.

- Put customers or clients at the heart of everything. They pay the wages!

CREATING A CUSTOMER SERVICE STRATEGY

> To me, success means happiness. I aim to have happy customers and put them at the heart of what we do. I also want happy staff who enjoy their work, respond to my requests, and who want to learn and reach their full potential — staff who realise they are the driving force behind providing excellent customer service and who get a buzz out of the rewards it brings.

On average, we spend about eight hours a day at work, so it is important that we enjoy what we do. Customers also prefer to buy from a business that is buzzing, and where the staff are happy and creating the right atmosphere. We are all in the business of selling a product or a service and the staff must be able to sell with passion. Happy employees are known to be more productive and will stay with a company longer, which means you will spend less on the recruitment and training of new staff.

However, the success of any business starts with the person at the top: how good they are at motivating, inspiring and developing their staff and how well they treat them. In a small business, this is even more important because the owner is usually visible to both the customers and the employees. If employers don't treat their staff in a way that they'd want to be treated themselves, how can they expect their businesses to survive? People work best when they are made to feel good about themselves and committed, well trained and happy staff will drive success.

A miserable boss will have miserable staff and unhappy customers. For example, there is a small independent shop in my local area where the owner never smiles. He always looks miserable and, as a customer, I feel I'm an interruption to his day. His staff — who are all young — reflect his attitude when dealing with customers and obviously have never had any training or guidance in customer service. Even though his products are of a good standard, I only ever shop there if I'm desperate. I wonder how long that business will struggle on for before it is forced to close?

Never underestimate how important good customer service is to the people you sell to, or want to sell to. Companies that recognise this will prosper and it will drive their business forward. Price does not seem to be the primary factor, as one might expect; although it does, of course, play a role, especially in an economic downturn when business is ever more competitive and customers more demanding but even in a recession customers definitely still want friendly, caring staff who offer consistently good service and products to match.

A customer who was enjoying lunch in my restaurant the other day was expressing his delight at the attention he was receiving from my staff, who were all smiling and appeared to be enjoying their work. He told me that he'd recently been to an expensive restaurant where the food was excellent but the staff were so miserable that he wouldn't be going back. His comment was that he would prefer to have food that was less elaborate as long as the atmosphere in the restaurant was relaxed and happy and that he was served by attentive and enthusiastic staff.

It is not just the friendly greeting and the 'enjoy your day' that pleases a customer — good customer service is about much more than that. Try to have fun with your customers and make them laugh. Customers will often forget what you say to them but will remember how you made them fell and it should involve everyone and everything in the organisation. Paul Howell of Unilever likens it to putting a man on the moon: the astronaut can't make the journey unless the engineer has tightened the nuts and bolts.

What does a customer service strategy aim to do?

All businesses should aim to provide excellent customer service and to give customers an experience to remember. To do this, you need to have a very clear vision of how your business is positioned in the market in which it operates and how you expect to reach your goals. Review your strategy regularly annually to make sure it's adapting to any changes in that market and continue to move your business forward.

As you create and implement your strategy, it's vital that everyone involved in the business knows about it, so that they understand what's expected of them. If your staff don't 'know their lines' — in every sense! — the business will definitely struggle, if not fail altogether.

I find it helpful to introduce some 'performance thinking' to get the business culture right: performers aim to please their audience, and that's what your company should be aiming to do for its customers. Maybe it's because of my professional dance background, but I believe that if you can think of business as 'just another performance', you have an advantage over some of your competitors, purely because performers are very focused and competitive and are only satisfied if they feel they have turned in an excellent result every day. Why not carry some of that energy and passion into your own company?

While it's important for you to take the lead and set the tone for how you want your business to be run, you must give employees the opportunity to challenge policies and practices. Ask them for their ideas about how the company can improve and continue to grow. Your staff are often more aware of customers' needs and buying trends than you, and they'll also perform better if they feel an integral and valuable part of the team. Their feedback is just as important as your customers so listen to them and make sure their contributions are taken seriously.

Think about your strengths and weaknesses

Many people find business jargon confusing and intimidating. I'm among them, although a few years ago I did pick up some very helpful tips. I won a competition to attend a course at the London Business School and one of the useful tools I discovered was a SWOT analysis, which examines your business's strengths, weaknesses, opportunities and 'threats' or challenges. It's a great way of looking at where you are now and where you want to be, and it will help you work out a strategy to get to your target.

While SWOT analyses *can* be extremely detailed and complex, they don't have to be. The following is a very simple example I did for The Cloud. Whatever industry you're in, however, it's *essential* that you are realistic about the positives and negatives that you have to work with: it's a complete waste of time if you get carried away!

Strengths

- My passion for the business and my communication skills.
- The hotel's excellent location.
- Targeting a niche market that is overlooked by many of our competitors.

■ Good staff retention — staff are encouraged to reach their full potential within the business.

Weaknesses

■ Lack of delegation in some areas.
■ Hiring the right staff (even though we retain staff well, recruiting the right people in the first place continues to be a major challenge for many small businesses, including mine).
■ Getting staff to accept and implement change.
■ Lack of parking space.

Opportunities

■ To increase our share of the niche market we target.
■ To build on our reputation for excellent customer care.
■ To win awards that raise our profile and reputation.
■ To provide a service that exceeds our customers' expectations and prove to them that our service exceeds a two-star rating.
■ To increase sales by developing new services that add value and make our services more attractive to our target market.
■ To move forward with new technology where appropriate.

Threats

■ Local competition.
■ Forces of nature or extreme weather conditions (floods, gales, snow) that would mean customers can't reach the hotel.
■ Bureaucracy — inspectors galore!

- Having a discontented customer who may put off other potential visitors.
- Food scares, fire, accidents at work.
- Bank rate and inflation.

Creating a real experience for your customers

While obviously the nitty-gritty of what your customers will want will depend very much on the industry in which you operate and the good and services you offer, there are some key rules that can apply to any business:

- Give a high-quality service and value for money.
- Tailor the services to your customers' specific needs (see below).
- Make sure your first point of contact is efficient and friendly: even if most of your inquiries come via the Internet, have an automated response that thanks people for contacting you, and which explains how quickly you'll be back in touch.
- If you say you'll contact customers within, say, two working days, stick to that promise, without fail.
- Be consistent and reliable in everything you do: use the best raw materials you can lay your hands on, deliver on time and on budget and if you do run into any problems, talk to the customer.
- Cater for, and be accessible to everyone, especially if they have mobility problems or other challenges. To tailor your website for use by those who have disabilities, visit the Web Accessibility Initiative's site at: http://www.w3.org/WAI/intro/accessibility.php

- Make sure the design, comfort and safety of your establishment is appropriate for your market.
- Deal with queries or complaints promptly and effectively, and keep relevant customers informed of their progress (see Chapter 9 for specific advice).
- If you sell any type of item that might benefit from after-sales care — machinery, IT or audio equipment, bicycles, cars — follow them up regularly to make sure your customers are happy.
- Continually strive to improve your services and look at your customers' needs (this applies to both internal and external customers, including staff and suppliers).

Making it personal

At The Cloud, we always aim to tailor our product and services to the customers' specific needs and, where possible, we try to *anticipate* their needs. For example, if we have elderly customers with mobility problems, we'll seat them near the door in the restaurant so that they don't have far to walk. During the summer months, the restaurant can be very hot and, owing to the nature of the building, we are not able to install air conditioning. If we notice that a customer is starting to look flushed, we give them a hand-held fan for their comfort. Realising that many of our younger customers enjoy the freedom of the New Forest National Park and bring their bikes with them we have now built a secure, covered bike shed for them to store their bikes safely overnight. It has been a great success and was an idea of one of my staff! We try and give customers more than they expect so that they leave the hotel having had a memorable experience. See Chapter 4 for more information on adding a personal touch.

Business is a battle, but one worth winning

Customers are increasingly demanding, encouraged by the media, and there may be days when it feels like the world is against you. However, no effort should be spared in pleasing the customer, as long as it's cost effective, regardless of how you are feeling or how the customer is behaving towards you.

Excellent customer service starts with the first contact a customer has with the organisation, whether it be by phone, e-mail, or in person. You only have one chance to make a good impression, so make sure that the relevant staff are friendly and efficient and that they are able to take decisions without having to defer to you. What would happen if you were not there?

Work on your welcome

I have very clear guidelines on how we respond to our customers at the hotel. Everyone is greeted at the door promptly with a smile and by name if possible. If they have a reservation for the restaurant, we take their coats and show them to a comfortable chair in one of the lounges where they can relax and look at the menu while enjoying a drink. This may sound very basic to most people but I'm always surprised, when I go out to eat, how often I have to either hang up my own coat or put it on the back of my chair and look for a member of staff to acknowledge I've arrived! I know the welcome we give to our customers keeps them coming back time and time again and it costs nothing.

Guests who arrive to stay in the hotel are greeted in the same way and, to make them feel welcome, the receptionist gives new customers a guided tour of the hotel so that they know how to find the restaurant and bar and feel comfortable in their new surroundings. We give them every piece of information we think they will need to help them to relax, before showing them to their room and helping them with their luggage. As they have often had a long and sometimes frustrating journey we offer our customers a complimentary tea or coffee and one of our chef's homemade biscuits on arrival, this is always well received by our guests. On their departure we give them a small bottle of water and homemade biscuit for their journey. Hopefully they will leave with a happy feeling as well as having received a warm welcome from us when they arrived. It's just another way of letting our customers know we care and hope that their overall experience from start to finish will make them want to return.

Little things really do make a difference, and that difference *does* matter. Guests are assured that if they need anything, they just have to let us know and we'll be happy to help. Being in the service industry, one would expect this attitude to prevail in all hotels and restaurants, but unfortunately it doesn't.

For example, when I arrived at a hotel in Devon last year, I had to wait to be checked in at reception. The young girl demanded my name in a most aggressive manner and, after taking down my details, she gave me the key to my room and told me the lift was down the corridor and that my room was on the first floor. There was no offer of a porter to help me with my luggage and I had to go up and down in the lift twice as I couldn't carry all my bags at once. I had a lot of books and my computer because I had decided to go away to this hotel to start writing the first edition of this book in peace and quiet! The receptionist just sat and watched me struggle. She certainly hadn't been made aware that a caring service and attitude give you a competitive edge and can increase your bottom line. Neither was she aware that I was about to write a book on customer service and she was providing me with some useful material! I haven't been back.

Answering the phone

The way the phone is answered at your company can win or lose you a customer. In a way, it's almost *more* important to make a good impression over the phone as the caller can't see your facial expression or body language, and so can only judge you by what you say and how you say it.

Being greeted by an answerphone message drives me mad. You're almost guaranteed to lose business that way, because if people have a query, they want to speak to a person, not an answering machine. It's a false economy to use one rather than employing somebody with excellent customer skills to answer the phone. Nothing annoys me more than leaving a message asking for somebody to return my call and waiting for up to several days before I get a reply. In the meantime, I've usually taken my custom elsewhere.

Always try to answer the phone within three rings if possible and speak clearly and enthusiastically. Try to smile while you're talking on the telephone, because experts say it makes you sound pleased to hear from the caller. I can judge a lot about an organisation from the attitude of the person answering my call and how they respond to my questions. It is one of my pet hates how few people know how to answer the phone in a friendly caring way and sound as if they are pleased to hear from me and I'm not an interruption to their day. We all know how exasperating it is to be left waiting on the phone for someone to respond to our call while listening to Act One of *Figaro*!

At The Cloud, staff are trained to answer the phone with: 'Good morning/evening, Cloud Hotel', putting the name of the business *after* the greeting. We have discovered that if you say the name of the establishment first, the caller invariably is not listening and will ask, 'Is that The Cloud Hotel?' Giving the name after the greeting when callers have tuned in to what you are saying avoids having to repeat it. Don't feel you have to say your name as well: the message gets too long. Just keep it simple, be straightforward and always end the conversation on a positive note (such as 'Thank you for calling'). Whatever you do, don't say 'Have a nice day' — it sounds so glib!

My staff are aware that everyone who phones or visits the hotel is a potential customer who may end up paying their wages. After all, even the men/women who deliver our laundry or vegetables have holidays and go out for meals so if they are treated the same way as the customers you have a good chance they will recommend you to their friends and family if not experience your product or service themselves. The challenge of my staff is to get a sale from every relevant call if possible. They need to listen carefully to the customer's request and give them as much information as possible about the hotel, the restaurant and the surrounding area to encourage the caller to book either a room or a table in the restaurant. Make a note of all relevant details about the customer that will help them to enjoy their experience with you and pass on any important information or messages to other members of the team if appropriate. Lack of communication among staff can cause a real breakdown in the process and affect the standard of customer service.

Recently I phoned a small family business that had been supplying me with electrical goods for years. I wanted to order some new televisions for the bedrooms. I had already bought ten from that shop, but wanted to order some more. The young assistant who answered the phone sounded half asleep, couldn't find my details on their database and told me to ring back another day! I have since discovered that this particular shop had just been sold and has new owners. If they want to compete with the big boys who can offer their products at a very competitive price, they are going to have to teach their staff some customer care skills in order to survive.

The reason I always used to shop at this particular establishment is that their customer service and follow-up were friendly and efficient and I had built up a relationship with them. As a customer, I like to be able to speak to a member of staff who is pleased to hear from me and who sounds passionate about their product. On this occasion, the shop assistant lost the new owners a sale of about £2,000. I wonder how much business he has lost from other customers? The new owners need to train their staff urgently!

Speed of service

In today's world, everything moves so quickly that speed of service is a winning formula. We are all in such a hurry to get what we want and when we want it, and it's the businesses that can supply their customers with their products or services promptly which survive. This does put a lot of pressure on businesses and the staff who have to deal with demand, but you just have to get on with it if you want to succeed: customers won't wait around! However, in a small business, you can't afford to have a member of staff available for every customer who walks through the door, so sometimes customers have to learn to be patient.

I'm amazed how often I see staff standing around idle in a small business. Have these businesses never heard of cost control? All I can say is they must have a very long shoestring! Staffing is one of the highest costs to any business and there has to be a balance between the cost to the business and the efficiency of the service. Getting the right balance can be very difficult to achieve but I have discovered that staff are usually happier and more productive when they are busy.

As long as customers who are waiting for service are acknowledged by a member of staff and told that someone will be with them as soon as possible, they're usually happy to wait. In situations like this, staff should use their initiative to seize every opportunity to try to please the customer, maybe by offering them a cup of coffee so that they can relax while they are waiting to be looked after. What really annoys customers, myself included, is being ignored.

Quality counts

High-quality service extends far beyond the friendly welcome and happy staff. It's the attention to detail and encompasses everything from how your products and services are presented to the customer, to the maintenance of the building and even down to how clean the loos are! This is an area that is so often overlooked, but you can be sure that most of your customers will use the facilities at some time and, if your loos aren't clean, what impression does that give? What is the cost to the business and what are the rewards? It doesn't take much to work out the benefits. So often businesses are busy investing a lot of money into advertising and marketing instead of investing in the quality of products they are offering.

Everything you do in a small business has to be cost-effective and it's essential that you plan and manage your cash flow carefully, according to the type of industry you work in. I control my spending very carefully but am continually investing in new furnishings and upgrading the facilities at my hotel as and when I can afford to.

Attractive surroundings have a positive psychological effect on people – customers and staff alike. Comfortable chairs, well-lit rooms and a pleasant décor are all part of the customer service strategy at The Cloud. As crucial as this is, however, I try to keep a tight rein on spending. I don't believe in major refurbishments where hundreds of thousands of pounds are spent – the money usually has to be borrowed and has to be paid back to the bank with interest. At the same time as you're paying back that loan, you also have to cover your everyday costs, including staffing, heating, supplies, business rates, licences and so on. This is where so many small businesses get into financial trouble, especially if they have not been in business long enough to have built up a strong customer base.

One of the best ways of keeping a handle on how the cash is flowing in and out of your business is to prepare regular financial reports. I find monthly ones work best for me, but assessing your finances weekly may be better for you. It depends how strong your financial situation is, but it is imperative that you do it regularly to be able to control your costs rigidly, delight your customers on a shoestring and delight yourself by making a profit!

I am always looking at ways I can reduce my overheads, as this is a great way to increase profit. I choose my suppliers carefully and always try to negotiate a better price from them. I keep my staff costs down without jeopardising my standards of customer service and I make sure there is as little waste as possible in the hotel. Watch carefully your so-called 'little expenses' as they can turn into big expenses if they get out of hand. Saving £50 a week on something may not seem a lot, but over the course of a year it will add up to more than £2,500. Buy energy efficient appliances: they not only reduce the use of natural resources and help to protect the environment, but also lower your energy and utility bills. The money saved could be invested in improving your services. Add that up over a period of time and you could have enough shoestrings to really grow your business.

I control my costs by not spending more than I need to but still maintaining high standards. I plan and manage my costs and I get my cash in fast! That way I have built a financially solid and stable business. Again, it is the small things that really do count and small savings in any business can make a huge difference.

3 MAKING A POSITIVE IMPRESSION

> I am a huge believer in the value of a smile. Think about it: when someone smiles at you, it almost always makes you feel better. If this is true for you, then it will be true for your customers.

I recently spent a day at a leisure park with my grandchildren. Although it was supposed to be a place of fun and enjoyment for the customers, it was very noticeable how miserable most of the staff looked. It certainly didn't seem to be a place of fun and enjoyment for them. A smile and a cheerful welcome would have made such a difference to our experience and enjoyment of the day.

Having the right attitude, along with strong leadership and training, can transform the fortunes of any company, large or small. You could argue that small businesses have many advantages over large corporations in terms of keeping their customers happy, and I'll be looking at these in more detail in Chapter 7.

We've all experienced good customer service, just as we've all been on the receiving end of poor customer service that has made us angry, frustrated and often determined never to give the company in question our business again.

When we talk about 'customer service', shops, hotels and restaurants are often the first businesses that spring to mind because they are in the service industry. As mentioned earlier, though, we're all customers in one form or another in most daily situations. When we visit the doctor or the dentist, we most likely aren't feeling too good, and being greeted by a receptionist with a smile and a friendly face can make us feel a lot better straight away.

Delivering excellent customer service is about a lot more than smiling, of course. It is your customers' *whole* experience of your company that will help them decide whether or not to use your product or services again. The most successful businesses are those where the employees are passionate about the business and leave at the end of the day feeling fulfilled and looking forward to going to work the next day, and whose customers leave the company wanting to do business with them again. Without happy customers, there is no profit, no jobs, no growth and, ultimately, no business. The customer should be your driving force, motivating you to give them a little more than they expect.

Customer-care guru Buzz Kennedy says that: 'I think that business practices would improve immeasurably if they were guided by "feminine" principles – qualities like love and care and intuition.' And I am inclined to agree.

Hiring the right people

Delighting your customers starts by employing the right people and then making sure that they're enjoying what they do: happy employees are a great first step towards creating happy customers. Your staff are your business's greatest assets, and unless they are content, confident and appreciated you won't get their full co-operation in making a success of your business. They are the 'front-liners', the people who deal directly with the customer and who can therefore make or break your business.

It's important that you set an example. Treat everyone — members of your team, your suppliers, your customers and all those who come into contact with your organisation — with care and respect, and the knock-on effect will be delighted customers. Respect is where customer CARE starts:

- **C**ommitment
- **A**ttitude
- **R**espect
- **E**nthusiasm

Hiring the right people, then, is incredibly important for any business, but even more so for small enterprises. Not only is it expensive and disruptive to have to keep recruiting new staff, but you also lose the knowledge, expertise and relationships that have built up over time. Getting your hiring policies right will have a very positive impact on the reputation and productivity of the company, and it can also boost the morale and efficiency of the whole team.

So where do you start? Firstly, think about whether you really need to recruit any new staff at all. Depending on the size of team you have working for you already, it might be that tasks could be spread among other people. However, don't be tempted to make false economies: if money is tight, you might be keen to save the money you spent on someone's salary and plough the cash back into the business. However, if it turns out that the job can't realistically be split between the rest of your team, you'll find that overall productivity will drop as people struggle to manage their increased workload.

If you decide that you do need to replace a departing employee or that the business is expanding and you need to fill a new position, you will have to draw up a job specification. This should list the skills, qualities and experience that the ideal candidate will have. Obviously these details will vary according to the type of industry, but as we're concentrating here on people who will be working with customers, candidates will at least need to have:

- **a cheerful disposition**
- **a good attitude**
- **good communication skills**
- **strong interpersonal skills**
- **the ability to solve problems**
- **the ability to work under pressure**
- **good telephone skills**
- **be IT literate**

You will no doubt think of more items to add to the list that are pertinent to your business. Draw them up into a basic grid or list so that by the time you come to interview your shortlist of candidates (see below), you have a fair system by which you can judge the interviewees. Below I list some basic points to look out for during interviews, but as employment law is so complex these days, I recommend that you seek detailed advice about recruitment to ensure that you comply with the law. The Business Link website (**www.businesslink.gov.uk**) has some useful information, and you could also discuss any queries with your solicitor.

Pre-interview

Although interviewing candidates to find the best person to fill the vacancy is the main part of the recruitment process, it's essential to put some work in well before that to make sure that you select the right candidates for interview. You must have a clearly worded job description, together with an idea of the skills, personality and experience necessary to do the job. This will give you a benchmark against which you can measure all the candidates that you'll be meeting.

Once you've advertised the position and received all the application forms or letters and CVs, the next step is to do an initial trawl to select a list of candidates for interview. To come up with a shortlist, I suggest you conduct some telephone interviews: they're a great way of finding out more about an applicant while at the same time judging just how good their telephone and general communication skills are. Social networking sites such as Facebook, Twitter, LinkedIn and blogs are a mine of information. It never ceases to amaze me how much personal information people post on public forums and I would suggest that employers would be well advised to research this resource before arranging an interview with a prospective candidate.

During the interview

There are many aspects to consider when you are interviewing for a vacant position.

As well as being physically and intellectually capable of doing the job, the ideal potential employee should be someone with good teamwork skills who could slot into the existing team structure relatively easily. I've often employed people on the basis of personality and who have a 'can do' attitude rather than qualifications. If they fit the role profile, I can teach the skills they need – but I can't change someone's personality or train them if they have a bad attitude!

I also look for someone who has made the effort to look their best for the interview, whatever position they are applying for. If you look good, you feel good about yourself and your confidence grows. I also pay close attention to their body language, as that will play a big role in how they relate to my customers. For example:

- How well do the candidates maintain eye contact?
- Do they display defensive body language, such as folded arms and crossed legs, when asked a question?
- Do they smile?
- Can they hold conversations?
- Have they researched the hotel and, if so, how much do they know about us?

I take particular note of the way an interviewee addresses me in that all-important first meeting. Being able to communicate in a friendly and confident manner without being over-familiar is an essential skill in customer care.

Keep an eye on the competition

When you're about to appoint someone to a role, think about the salary and benefits you can offer him or her. Read the local newspapers and trade magazines and see what other businesses are offering in their advertisements. Seeing what other businesses require can also alert you to changes that are taking place in your industry and which may be worth investigating.

Post-interview tactics

When you're ready to make the final selection, always take up references. It's unlikely that a small business will have a human resources department to make in-depth enquiries, and you can't rely solely on references, but aim to find out as much information as possible as to whether your candidates are as good as they seem on paper or at interview and whether they have all the qualities and the attitude necessary for the role. It really is worth putting in the time and effort to get the recruitment process right as you should be looking long term and the knock-on effects can be huge if you get it wrong.

If you hire the wrong person, not only can they upset your customers and your team, but they can also cost you a lot of money. If you don't retain your staff, the cost of training will only be beneficial to the next employer. Recruitment is one of the biggest costs in business, so if you have to constantly replace staff, it will affect the bottom line and soak up a lot of valuable time, too.

So now you've chosen the best candidate, the references all look fine, and you're ready to go. Once the person has accepted your offer, do let the unsuccessful candidates know. If it was a close-run contest and you'd like to keep in touch with any of the interviewees, ask for their permission to keep their CV or application form on file.

The magic question

How do you know if you are about to hire the right person? To be honest, there's no way you *can* know until that person has been working for you for several weeks. For that reason, make sure you have a probation period in place so that if things aren't working out, you can go your separate ways after three or six months and make this clear *at the start* of the recruitment process; don't just spring it on them at the last minute as this could have legal implications and prove to be both expensive and damaging.

My decision to take someone on as an employee is usually very much based on my instincts as well as that all-important first impression. In a small company, however, with its inevitably small and often close-knit team, it is often a good idea to involve other key members of staff in the final stages of the interview process. Their opinions could be invaluable in making the final decision about the compatibility of the potential new member of staff.

Integrating a new member of staff into the team

When you replace a valued member of staff, there is often a tendency to compare the new person with the member of staff who has left. This can be demotivating for everyone involved: there's nothing worse than being introduced as 'the new X'. There is a positive side, though, in that new people bring new ideas and often inject the organisation with a much-needed dose of fresh enthusiasm.

To get new recruits off to the best possible start in your business, make sure that they fully understand their duties and responsibilities and the way you want it done. It's also important that everyone carries out their duties in the same way and to the same high standard that is expected from them. (This is where the job description you drew up earlier in the recruitment process will be so valuable.) If possible, arrange for their starting date to overlap with the leaving date of the departing employee, so that he or she can explain exactly what the job entails on a day-to-day basis. This is also a good opportunity for the new person to be introduced to any key suppliers and customers, which should help get their relationship off to a good start.

Do make sure that new staff are aware of the overall vision of your business. Don't assume that people will magically 'know' what you want them to do and where you want your company to be in two years' time. Why would they? They're not telepathic. Remember, you have probably been doing this for years and it is almost second nature by now, but for newcomers it will be very different. Use the induction process as an opportunity to think long and hard about the impression that your business gives and to reassess your plans for the future if you need to.

Some larger organisations have a mentoring system that gives new recruits a point of contact in the business, someone with whom they can speak about any queries or concerns they have. Small businesses often don't have the resources to do this, but if your business is growing quickly, it's certainly an idea to bear in mind. The Coaching and Mentoring Network has some useful information online at: www.coachingnetwork.org.uk/resourcecentre/WhatAreCoachingAndMentoring.htm

Building the perfect team

You may never find the perfect person for the job in hand, but you can put together a really great team, no matter how different the personalities involved, and this is summed up neatly by the Japanese proverb, 'None of us is as smart as all of us'. To build a successful team, it's hugely important that each individual member of staff feels a sense of pride and ownership in the company. Working towards a common goal can bring a team closer together and enable them to perform more effectively. The good thing about a team is you have others on your side and a good team can separate the winners from the losers.

Business turnaround expert, Sir John Harvey-Jones, suggests that: 'The ideal organisation, and the one with the best chance of success, is one where if you ask anyone, from the chairman down to the newest recruit on the shop floor, what the business is trying to do, you would get the same answer.' To produce a balanced and motivated team, each individual needs to be able to work effectively with their colleagues. To achieve that, each person must know exactly what is expected of him or her within the organisation.

A balanced team consists of a combination of team leaders, who are ambitious and drive the business forward, and 'background' workers who are reliable and happy to do the smaller, everyday jobs that are the bedrock of any business. It is important, though, that the background workers feel as important and as valued as the leaders, and that they are rewarded equally. If this doesn't happen, a team's morale can plummet.

It's true, of course, that small companies can't always afford to compete with the larger organisations in terms of salaries and bonuses, but financial rewards aren't always the primary driving force for people. I'm not suggesting, of course, that people are happy to work for free, but in a small company, recognising a job well done, making that person feel valued and special and, above all, thanking them for their time and effort can help make up for smaller monetary rewards, and motivate your team to achieve even greater things. There are so many ways to reward your staff and show your appreciation with very little cost to the company, such as:

- offering your staff flexible working hours
- celebrating particular achievements
- organising staff outings
- remembering and celebrating birthdays and other special events

Most small businesses in the UK employ are owned and staffed by the same person, but if your company employs a number of people, make sure that there is a clear staffing structure, so that people know to whom they should report (if it's not you) on a daily basis.

I'm a firm believer that the overall attitude of a company or business comes from the top. If the person at the top of a company has a bad attitude and is always complaining, more often than not this trickles down through the ranks of the staff, who then mirror this behaviour, resulting in unhappy customers. If the leader is happy, enthusiastic, hard-working, energetic and passionate about the business, then the staff are more likely to adopt this attitude.

Training staff

I am passionate about training. It's not just about sending a member of your staff on a one-day jolly (although that can be a real boost to motivation); it should be an ongoing process, starting on the day that a member of staff joins you and ending when he or she leaves. You will find that most people are keen to increase their skills and knowledge if they're given the chance. There is, however, no point in training your staff — and encouraging them to grow and develop — if you don't give them the opportunity to use their new-found skills. For this reason, it's important to learn to delegate and to trust your staff. They are more likely to feel fulfilled and valued if you respect their judgement, and their confidence and ability will grow as a result.

By supporting your staff as they broaden their skills, you'll help them to discover new talents. In turn, they will be able to train and encourage new members of staff, thereby helping to create an organisation where everyone can flourish and grow. Nothing creates tiredness and lack of interest more than boredom in the workplace: if people are bored and apathetic, their concentration will lapse and mistakes will happen. The added benefit of this approach is that *you'll* have more time to dedicate to building your business if you know that you can rely on your team to deal with all the day-to-day running of affairs.

Training doesn't have to be expensive, but any money wisely invested in this area should result in a profitable return. It's not the cost of training but the lack of training that affects the bottom line. This can be difficult to measure, but do think about the potential benefits it could bring to your business. For instance, one of your staff might want to attend a course to develop their negotiating or IT skills.

Only you can decide the type of training that's most appropriate for your business. As I have a service industry background, my staff training always starts with appearance — how someone dresses and presents themselves. Good appearance breeds self-esteem. Remember, customers can tell a lot about you from your body language, so my training also includes deportment: no hands in pockets, no leaning on counters and always looking alert even if you have had a late night. However harsh it may sound, I always tell my staff to remember that customers are not interested in their personal problems. Guests have come away to have a break from their own lives and problems and do not need to be confronted by the details of someone else's!

I recently went into my local branch of a well-known chain of coffee shops for a coffee and snack. Having so many demands on my time and attention, I was looking forward to relaxing and enjoying an uninterrupted cup of coffee and a quiet moment away from my work. Full of anticipation, I joined the end of a short queue that was being regaled with a catalogue of woes by a young woman serving behind the counter. 'Oh God, today has been awful already. I don't know what's the matter with me. I'm not normally like this. The sandwiches turned up late, we didn't have enough milk, I spilt coffee over the floor . . .' And so on. Now, we all feel like this at times and I'm the first one to admit I'm no Pollyanna, but when we go into a restaurant, cafe, hotel or coffee shop, we want to get away from our everyday worries and enjoy some 'me' time before we face the world again.

I was looking for a bit of peace. I did get my cup of coffee in the end, but my visit was marred from the very beginning by having to listen to a stranger's moans about her less than perfect day. As a customer, you don't want to spend money to listen to someone whingeing – you can have that all at home or in the office for free.

Once again, I can highlight the direct parallels between business and theatre. Just as you wouldn't want to see a show where the performers were banging on about sore feet, so you don't want to go for a coffee, a meal or even shopping and listen to the person serving you telling you what a bad day they have been having.

First impressions really do count, even more so in the hospitality industry. It is a fact that people remember what they see much more than what they hear. Members of my staff are therefore instructed to look clean and tidy at all times. Their uniforms should be ironed, long hair tied back and shoes polished. Everyone at my hotel has a uniform that is suitable for their duties, and they are expected to wear it with pride. They are representing my business, and ultimately this means that they are representing me. If you present yourself well to your customers, you will gain their confidence straight away.

If the first impression is visual, the second is auditory. Whether you're speaking to a customer in person or on the phone, greet them clearly and confidently. Make sure that your voice conveys to the customer that you are pleased to either see or hear from them. It amazes me how little time is taken to train staff in the basic skills of communication. It costs nothing to explain to staff why slang words, such as 'hi', rather than a polite 'good morning/evening', are not an appropriate greeting, why customers do not want to hear swearing, and how the way they speak to each other has a knock-on effect to the customer.

Ultimately it is the business that suffers for the bad attitude of their staff. Of course, there is always the chance that these staff do not feel valued, and so see no reason to put themselves out. In other words, they are completely demotivated. If you feel that is the case in your business, act now to sort it out. Show the type of leadership that can turn things round. Remember, as a small company, you have an advantage in that your team works closely together and you should be able to communicate with each other clearly and regularly.

Front-liners

The staff members who meet the customers first — waiters/waitresses, shop assistants, receptionists, delivery men/women, for example — are key to those important first impressions. These 'front-liners' are essential to the success of the business and have a huge responsibility for the reputation of the company. More often than not, though, they receive lower wages than do the management staff.

These front-liners can make or break your business, so it is imperative that you employ the right people for these positions and that you train and motivate them properly. A lot of this training can be done in-house (you probably do it every day without realising), but you could also investigate specific training courses if your budget allows. Remember to keep all training focused and to check that it will have a demonstrable value to the business, so that you see some return on your investment.

I once changed my laundry supplier because the delivery man was rude to me on several occasions. His response to the news that I had given my business to another company was: 'Good. That's one less call I'll have to make'. It didn't seem to occur to him that if other people also decided to change supplier because of his attitude, he might end up without a job!

His attitude may not have been entirely his fault, though. Perhaps no one had explained to him how important it is to treat the customer with respect. Maybe he was overworked and tired and did not feel valued by his boss. Everyone wants to be appreciated, to feel important and get some form of approval for their work. Constant criticism can take away our confidence and motivation, as well as making us defensive and resentful towards our employers. If that delivery man did not feel a sense of shared ownership of the business, he would not see why he should make an effort to please the customer. If the owner or manager is passionate about their business, that enthusiasm should rub off on to the people around them, staff and customers alike.

It's often the case that larger organisations take the front-liners for granted. In this particular case, the net result was that they lost several thousand pounds-worth of business from my hotel alone.

Customer care is all about forging good, open relationships. It's two-way traffic:

- staff need to be sensitive to the needs of their customers, treat them appropriately and communicate effectively
- customers need to treat employees with respect if they wish to be shown respect too!

4 ADDING A
PERSONAL TOUCH

To have your own company, be able to compete in your market and be successful, you have to live, eat and sleep the business and give it all you've got. This can put pressure on your personal life, especially if you're trying to juggle family and work, and even more so if you are a single parent and the breadwinner.

This is the situation I found myself in when my husband died and I had to take over the running of the hotel. Overnight I had to think like an entrepreneur and wear many 'hats' at once. But one of the advantages of owning your own business is that you have the power to choose, control and direct your own destiny — it is much easier for you to get to know your customers and for them to get to know you.

Tell your own story

One excellent way of developing a relationship with your customers is to tell them about yourself. It's even better if you have an interesting story to tell, because they'll want to get to know you! If you can add a touch of glamour, so much the better. I've been very lucky in that respect, because being a former Tiller Girl raises my profile and is a wonderful marketing tool for my hotel.

For readers under the age of 50, the Tiller Girls were a troupe of dancers, famous for their precision and high-kicking routines. As I mentioned earlier, every week we appeared on the TV variety show *Sunday Night at the London Palladium*. It was the ambition of every performer to appear at the Palladium and I was fortunate to work with many British and American stars, including Judy Garland, Cliff Richard, Shirley Bassey and, of course, the host of the show, Bruce Forsyth.

Before I joined the Tiller Girls, I worked in shows all over the UK and know most British cities by the theatres I've appeared at. My customers travel from all over the UK to my hotel, and having some knowledge about where they've come from enables me to talk to them about their local area and share experiences. It's a great way of breaking the ice and building a rapport with my customers.

I loved every minute of my dancing career and I now put that energy and enthusiasm into running my business. One of the first commercial lessons I learned was from Bob Paton, a successful American restaurateur whom I met at a conference for small businesses. He told me there are three things you must remember to be successful:

1. Be good at what you do and enjoy it.
2. Be unique.
3. Tell the world about it.

I've always tried to follow this advice, and Bob's third point, 'Tell the world about it', has probably been the most influential to me. While it's important to focus on the future, I've found that my customers, mainly the older ones, love to hear about my days on the stage: it's some nostalgia for them and an opportunity for me to tell them more about the hotel. Sometimes they even bring their friends to meet me, which spreads the news about The Cloud further and introduces me to more potential new customers. Even the younger customers love to hear about my dancing days: a spot of show business never fails to engage people of any age! Be proud of your achievements and don't be embarrassed to 'tell the world'. Remember the words of Nelson Mandela in his inaugural speech in 1994 (taken from *A Return to Love* by Marianne Williamson):

> Our deepest fear is not that we are inadequate.
> Our deepest fear is that we are powerful beyond measure.
> It is our light, not our darkness that most frightens us.
> We ask ourselves, 'Who am I to be brilliant, gorgeous, talented and famous?'
> Actually, who are you not to be?

These are some of the most powerful and inspiring words I have heard. So share your successes with your customers and your staff. Blow your own trumpet and build up a secure and trusting relationship with them.

Mark special occasions

Business life can be pretty tough and stressful, so I make a point of celebrating every achievement, anniversary and birthday at The Cloud. It's a great way to boost morale and keep everyone's motivation strong. Nothing goes unnoticed if I can help it.

For example, whenever customers make a booking for lunch or dinner in the restaurant, it's our policy to ask if they're marking a special occasion. If they're celebrating a birthday, we make sure they have a personalised card waiting for them at their table. At the end of the meal, the staff present them with a small birthday cake with our compliments and everyone sings 'Happy Birthday'. They then have the choice of enjoying the cake with their coffee or taking it home. Of course, there are some customers who ask us not to serenade them as they don't like a fuss (I didn't think our singing was that bad, but we respect their wishes), but it's important to make a big effort to make your customers feel valued, appreciated and to create an intimate, positive and long lasting relationship with them.

Anniversaries are also recognised with a card and small box of chocolates. The cards are printed specially for us and feature a photo of the hotel on the front. Not only does it delight the customer at being made to feel special, but it also adds a personal touch and a memorable experience of their visit to the hotel and the card is a useful keepsake of that. We try to change the photo on the card regularly as so many of our customers come to celebrate their birthday or wedding anniversary with us every year. It becomes a tradition. The cost to us is minimal compared to the rewards it brings.

The hospitality industry probably offers more opportunities to spoil customers than some other industries, but whatever business you're in, think about what you can do to keep your customers coming back. If they're delighted with the service and personal treatment you've given them, they will likely tell their friends.

Customers are walking advertisements for your business and you can reduce your advertising costs considerably by obtaining positive feedback from them. Research has shown that word of mouth is between one thousand and five thousand times more powerful than conventional advertising. Advertising costs can be a major outlay for small businesses, and I control my advertising budget very carefully. I will only consider placing an advert in a magazine if they are prepared to combine it with an editorial feature. Editors are always on the look-out for news and stories to fill their pages, so it's always worth getting in touch with them. The rewards from an editorial far exceed the response to a run-of-the-mill advert alongside many others. Some interesting advice I received from an Editor of a local evening newspaper recently was that you are more likely to have your press release noticed if you send it by post. The newspaper receives hundreds of e-mails every day and they just scan through them whereas you have a better chance of having a letter noticed and read and subsequently your news published.

I take every opportunity to keep in touch with my customers, and Christmas is no exception. We send a Christmas card to everyone who has stayed at the hotel during that calendar year, along with a letter from me thanking them for their custom and letting them know of any special events coming up over the next 12 months. The letter is enclosed in the card with a note of the following year's prices.

The card has a photo of the hotel or the staff so that we're uppermost in customers' minds, and we put a lot of effort into planning and producing the card. As the photo has a Christmas theme, it usually has to be taken in the previous year while the Christmas decorations are still up. I send out about two thousand cards a year: yes, it is a big job, but the rewards and repeat business it produces far exceed the time and money we spend on it. It reminds our customers that we are still in business.

As we have a database of all our customers' names and addresses, it is relatively easy for us to do this kind of promotion. If you work in retail, though, and don't have this information, you could get round it by slipping a Christmas greeting or card into the carrier bag with the product your customer has just bought to make him or her feel special and valued.

Celebrate your company's achievements

Your internal customers are just as important as your external ones, and they need praise and recognition, too. It's not unheard of for a customer to be enjoying some morning coffee in one of our hotel lounges and to hear the 'pop' of a champagne cork and some laughter coming from the kitchen area. The staff may be celebrating an award we've won or somebody's birthday but, whatever the occasion, I make sure we recognise everyone's contribution to the success of the business and that I praise them personally. There is nothing better for a business to be able to impress customers than an award either for the company or for a particular member of staff's achievements. Never miss an opportunity to promote any success stories.

Every year, I take my staff to a show in London's West End, followed by dinner, to thank them for their hard work and loyalty and, of course, to further nurture a sense of team spirit. The cost to the business? A few bottles of champagne, a hired coach, theatre tickets and dinner. The rewards? Staff who feel valued and remain a member of staff (as I have found) for many years.

Spreading the word

In 2006, I celebrated 30 years in business by throwing a dinner party and invited a mix of regular customers, friends, long-standing staff, suppliers, my maintenance team and, of course, my bank manager, without whose help in the early days I wouldn't be running The Cloud today! The evening would not have been complete without my four children, five grandchildren and my mother joining in the celebrations.

I invited a local magazine to come and take photos of the evening's celebrations and they were printed in the next issue. The magazine in question has a very large distribution over a wide area and I was delighted with the free publicity we received. Because the business was seen to have a personal story and a human element, people were interested in finding out more about The Cloud.

Newsletters

A newsletter is another cost-effective way of spreading information about your business. We print two newsletters a year and we mainly cover any future charity events that we are organising. For example, we always take part in the World's Biggest Coffee Morning to raise money for Macmillan Cancer Support. We don't miss any opportunity to promote achievements or interesting news about my staff, my customers and myself. Do check with the people you feature – customers and staff – and make sure they're happy to be included before you go ahead. Never disclose any confidential or personal information that they might be unhappy about.

Essentially, our newsletters tell stories and our customers love reading them. Customers will personally congratulate a member of staff for an achievement reported in the newsletter. That recognition has a wonderful positive effect on the members of staff involved; it raises their self-esteem and makes them feel valued, gives them an opportunity to chat to the customers and often get some useful feedback that everyone can benefit from.

We enclose a newsletter with each brochure we send out to customers and also leave some at reception so that anyone can pick one up and take it away to read later if they so wish. The aim is to distribute them far and wide and to attract new customers as well as retain our regular customers' interest in the business. Although I have my newsletters printed professionally, you don't have to go to that expense if money is tight. If you have an eye for design (or know someone who has), it's fine to design and print them yourself – it's the content that is important.

Remember to:

■ **Write for your reader, not yourself.** Don't write long screeds of text: people have very short attention spans, so write short paragraphs that contain the key points you want to get across.

- **Do a draft first.** Once you've finished the draft, put it aside for a few hours and then come back to it with a fresh eye. Take out any repetition.
- **Keep it simple.** Avoid jargon and overly complicated language, even if your business operates in a technical industry. New customers, who do not have your knowledge, may be put off by what looks complicated.
- **Illustrate, if you can.** Thanks to digital cameras and software packages, it's easier than ever to take photographs and include them in printed material. Make sure that any photos you use have a high enough resolution to be seen clearly — aim for 300dpi for optimum clarity.
- **Include your contact information.** If the newsletter gets passed on by an existing customer to a friend or family member who doesn't know you or your business, they can't get in touch if they don't have a phone number, e-mail or postal address by which to contact you.
- **Read the text carefully for spelling mistakes or grammatical errors before you have the final version printed.** Ideally, ask a friend or colleague to read it for you: they're more likely than you to spot mistakes, as you'll have seen the text many times by this point!

E-mails

E-mails can be one of your best marketing assets and they are an ideal way of passing on information to existing customers. They're a cost-effective way to market any special offers and to make sure that people don't forget you. I certainly find that when I get a message from a company whose products or services I've enjoyed, my memory is jolted and I think about using that company again. We ask every customer for their e-mail when we are checking them into the hotel. Some customers prefer not to give it to us which we respect. It's their choice, but we *make absolutely sure* that we have the permission of the customers who have provided us with their e-mails to send them messages electronically: unsolicited e-mails are spam. Avoid sending them at all costs. Always give people the opportunity to unsubscribe, although you have received their permission to send e-mails sometimes they change their mind and can become irritated by them.

When you're composing an e-mail, remember to:

- **Create an attention-grabbing subject line** that conveys both who you are (so that readers aren't puzzled) and what your big idea is — 'Spring Offers from Quinn Cycles' or 'Buy Early for Christmas at Harris Crafts'.
- **Keep it brief.** People tend to scan e-mails (even newspaper editors!) and websites quickly rather than take their time reading them, so keep paragraphs short. Put a link to your website that readers can click on, so they can find extra details or information.
- **Make it easy to read.** Highlight important words or phrases in bold or a different colour so that they stand out clearly when people are scanning. Some people find long stretches of italic text hard to read, so avoid that if possible.
- **Don't send big attachments.** They'll clog up your customers' inboxes. Again, put a link into your e-mail so that people can click through if they wish.
- **Give people an incentive.** Create a sense of 'urgency' so that people are prompted to take up the special offer you're e-mailing about. 'Buy before 30th November to get free

postage and packaging', for example, or 'Book by 31st July to take advantage of our special weekend rate'.

Blogs

A blog is a very useful and effective way of communicating your news, special offers or events in the area to your customers or in fact, to millions of people all over the world. It can also have links to useful websites. It is a journal or diary that is available on the web where you can update genuine information as regularly as you choose with personal news, events and business news. Adding a picture or photo connected to your current blog can create more interest. A blog contains loads more information than a website and should be regularly updated. It also allows readers to post comments, subscribe and to be able to receive notification of a new article posted on your blog. To increase readership for your blog include a link to it at the end of e-mails.

Twitter

This is another way of keeping in regular touch with your customers with simple short, bite-size updates using up to 140 characters. It's primarily used for conversation connecting you with a great number of people and can create many opportunities for your business. 170 million tweets are sent everyday from Twitter across the world giving even small companies the opportunity to listen to and become closer to their customers.

LinkedIn

This is the world's leading online network for professional people. LinkedIn gives people the opportunity to promote themselves and connect with other like-minded professionals where people can connect and network with each other.

Facebook

The growth of Facebook over the last few years is incredible with over five million active users worldwide. It is a great way to share news, events, special offers and experiences with family, friends and customers.

Apps

Apps [for 'applications'] are a time saving way of communicating your business efficiently. With the ever popularity of smart phones and portable tablet devices (such as the iPad) apps have become an invaluable way of promoting your business efficiently whilst communicating and engaging with current and potential clients/customers.

Social media and technology have changed the way people are communicating with each other and in particular, the way in which businesses are reaching out to their customers and developing new markets, all at very little cost.

Remember that anything you put online can be seen by an extremely wide audience and will remain there for a long time so be careful what you write about yourself or your business! I find it can be incredibly time consuming so you need to decide what is suitable for your business and be sure to keep it up to date and topical.

Acknowledging feedback

I always reply personally to every letter I receive from customers. Fortunately, most of them thank me and my staff for the great service and enjoyable time they've had at The Cloud.

In many businesses, it tends be just letters of complaint that receive a response, but I believe it's very important to acknowledge and respond to every letter and personal e-mail and to thank the sender for taking the trouble to get in touch with you. It helps to build a lasting customer relationship and makes it easier for you to stay in touch with them. If you respect people and treat them in a courteous manner, you will discover they will respond in kind and remain a loyal customer. Even letters of complaint should be answered in a positive manner, because the way you deal with these challenges could actually win the complainant round and turn him or her into a new or repeat customer, too. We'll look at how to deal with customer complaints in more detail in Chapter 9.

'Study' your customers

We all love to be recognised by staff when we go into a business, even though we may not admit it! Being addressed by name makes us feel valued and it enhances our perception of that company. It would be impossible to remember everyone's name, of course, but giving them a warm welcome is a great way of making them feel special, as is remembering their likes and dislikes.

By now you should have the technical facilities to build up reliable data about your customers' preferences so that you can further tailor your service to them. If you want to build intimate links with your customers you cannot afford to fall behind in understanding today's electronic technology. At The Cloud it allows us to keep a record of which newspaper each guest reads, so that when he or she returns back, we can ask if they'd like *The Times/ Guardian/ Daily Telegraph* again. We also keep a record of our guests' favourite rooms, so that if they make a repeat booking, we try to give them that room again, if they have an allergy or are 'gluten free' we make a note so we can inform the chefs. The opportunities to keep in touch with your customers and their requirements have never been better. As we have a computerised booking system, we can note these on-screen.

Studying your customers and remembering what pleases them is almost a career in itself, but it certainly can increase your profit. If people feel welcome, they'll come back.

Giving presentations and speeches

Remember the 'tell the world' theme from the beginning of the chapter? One good way of telling your story is to speak publicly to a live audience. Local business associations are always looking for speakers who have an engaging tale to tell, and it really is worth conquering any nerves and having a go. It's a great way of attracting new customers as well as potential new business partners or suppliers.

I used to be incredibly nervous about giving presentations, but practice has definitely helped me and I now feel very comfortable telling others about The Cloud and what we aim to do there. Talking about your business with passion will get the audience on your side early on and it can be inspiring for others to hear about business success stories too. I regularly speak at events held by Everywoman, a women's business organisation. Their conferences are attended both by established business owners and those thinking about taking the plunge and starting their own business, and I find it rewarding to feel I've played some part in helping others realise that they can make a success of their company.

By speaking publicly to local associations I've gained many new customers. It's helped put The Cloud on the map and, after listening to me, people feel they know me personally and that encourages them to be a customer. It makes them feel involved.

However successful you might feel you are, you can never afford to be complacent and there are always new customers to be won. Nearly everyone who runs a business has an interesting story to tell, whether it's about a past career, how a business was built to be successful or how a crisis was overcome. Whatever it is you've lived through or accomplished, have the courage to tell your story; there really is no better way of getting attention for your business, so get out of your comfort zone and do it! Members of the audience may tell your story to their friends and so the word spreads. Therefore, not only can it win you customers but you may also even get paid for it — a true win-win situation!

When you prepare your presentation, remember to:

- **research well.** Some people speak wonderfully off the cuff, but most of us need to do some homework beforehand. Ask the organisers of the event you're speaking at to give you some information about the audience so that you can target your talk to them and their needs. I always ask the average age of the audience and how many people they expect to be in the audience.
- **think about timing.** Find out how long you'll be speaking for and make sure that you stick to that limit. It's much better to leave people wanting to know more (and they can ask you questions afterwards anyway) rather than droning on for hours.
- **plan.** Work out what key points you want to get across and then structure the bulk of your presentation around them. Taking some notes as prompts is a good idea: don't write the whole thing out as you'll be tempted to read it out, rather than speak more fluently, but having some bullet points on small cards is a good back-up.
- **practise!** You'll feel a lot more confident about talking to others if you practise first. Ask a family member, friend or colleague to listen to you as you do a run-through. They'll be able to give you some useful feedback, and they can also time you so you know how things are panning out.

When you actually give your presentation:

- **don't speak too quickly.** It is very common to speak faster than you usually do when you're nervous, but try to keep things at a normal pace so that everyone can follow what you're saying.
- **stand up straight.** Good posture will make you look and feel more confident.
- **be enthusiastic.** If you can't speak with passion about your business, who can? Be proud of what you've achieved and let your commitment shine through to inspire and motivate others.
- **smile!** Your audience will respond to you better if you look as if you're glad to be talking to them.

One of my favourite quotes is:

> 'Be who you are,
> And say what you feel,
> Because those who mind don't matter,
> And those who matter don't mind.'
>
> *Dr Seuss*

A winning formula

Having consistently high standards and giving good old-fashioned personal service to customers is a winning formula for everyone:

- **customers** win because they are made to feel special and enjoy the quality treatment they receive;
- **members** of staff win because their job satisfaction will increase;

■ **the business** wins because you retain existing customers and gain new ones through word-of-mouth recommendations.

Write a Book

What better way is there to put you and your business on the map and to communicate with your customers than to write a book, as I am doing now! It can either be a book about your personal story or a subject you are passionate about but either way you will be a published author!

Your customers are your biggest asset and you want your business to be their first choice. If you go out every day with a positive attitude and are striving for perfection, you're much more likely to delight them.

5 CREATIVITY AT WORK

Einstein said: 'Imagination is more important than knowledge'. However, knowledge is incredibly powerful – and empowering – so if you can combine the two, you'll stand a very good chance of not only developing a very creative life but a creative and successful business as well.

Harnessing creativity

A creative mind can increase sales but only if your imagination and your knowledge, both of your business and your customers, are applied in a way that differentiates your business from your competitors'. Have the courage to try something new: competition is so fierce these days that you have to stand out from the crowd. You need to be noticed! Again I can draw a similarity to my previous career as a dancer: most dancers start their career in the chorus line, but to move on, they have to create an image and a talent that gets noticed, so that someone notices them and realises their potential.

So what can you and your business offer that's unique? It could be a hobby, the location of your business, a past career or any awards that you or your staff have won. If you have any of these assets, market them like mad. For example, a few years ago I was persuaded to promote my past career as a Tiller Girl and to display some of the photos I'd kept of those days in the hotel. To be honest,

I was apprehensive about this at first, but then by chance I met an interior designer who was just launching a new business. She was keen to get her new business recognised and to promote it. As a result, she agreed to theme my bar and redesign it at a very competitive rate and I was able to promote her business in return.

The timing was perfect, as I was aiming to boost the hotel's profile at that time, too, and we had great fun working together. The Tiller Bar (as it's now called) attracts a lot of attention from our guests, and it also brings in new customers who want to see the photos of the dancers and the stars of the Sixties that are displayed on the walls. The bar area itself is designed like a theatre proscenium arch and the curtains are draped to represent a stage. At night, we close the bar with a blind designed as a safety curtain that we pull down. It's unique to my hotel! There is also a scrapbook in the bar of my career featuring signed photos of the many celebrities I have worked with, my contracts, old programmes and some press cuttings of shows I have appeared in.

We've even created some Tiller-themed cocktails with names such as 'High Kicks', 'Curtain Call' and 'Tiller Thriller'. A customer had the great idea of our making postcards with a photo of a reunion of the Tiller Girls that took palce at The Cloud to sell in the hotel. I duly took up his suggestion and the postcards have also proved an excellent marketing tool, too. The interest it creates amongst my customers, both young and old, is astonishing. It is a talking point and leads to good customer relationships. Of course, I have to be prepared to spend time chatting to customers about it, which can divert me from other chores, but putting time in to communicate with my customers and buildind a good relationship with them means that they're more likely to keep coming back, so I will reap further benefits.

Each week I hold a small cocktail party in The Tiller Bar to welcome and to meet the guests. This gives the guests (my customers) the opportunity to chat to me and the staff, and get to know the other guests who are staying. It breaks down any shyness and helps create a friendly atmosphere and, sometimes, life long friendships between the customers. In fact, I have several couples who originally met at The Cloud and who now return every year at the same time to meet up. People love the theatre and find it intriguing, so we are never short of conversation with our customers at The Cloud. Despite my initial fears, making my former career a focus for marketing was one of the best ideas ever suggested to me and has really helped to put The Cloud on the map!

So ask yourself: 'What have I done that is different and unique to either myself or my business?' and 'Where could I create an interesting focus for my customers that will promote my business?' People are naturally curious and like to hear other people's stories: it's human nature, so tap into that. And don't think you have to spend a fortune on it: sometimes all it needs is a few photos on the wall and a scrapbook, yet the rewards can be very productive. Think 'simple but effective'. When you are running a business it is so easy to get bogged down with the everyday mundane tasks that you often neglect this aspect of customer service. So create some time to do it. NOW!

Focus on your unique selling points. Everyone has something special they are able to market and sell, so use your imagination. Sometimes I ask my friends, family and staff for ideas and suggestions that I might introduce into my business. I read books, magazines, autobiographies of successful business people and I love discovering how they achieved their goals. As long as you have a vision and goals – and that you're clear about what those goals are – there's no limit to what you can achieve with the right attitude. I'm a great believer in being positive even when everyone around you is negative. I avoid negative people, they drain your energy and crush your dreams. Positive attitudes create positive people and positive people create positive results.

We are all creative in different ways, so don't panic if you're not a great artist or writer: in business, creativity is about more than that. It's about looking at the opportunities and challenges that you face and thinking about how you can solve them in a way that's unusual, effective and customer-friendly. Finding a wonderful new way of tackling an issue is very invigorating, but do make sure, before you implement it, that it will have a positive impact on your bottom line.

Try to approach every area of your business with a creative 'hat' on and find ways of doing things differently from your competitors so that you will be the one who gives the five-star service and wins the customers. Every new day presents you with opportunities and the trick is to recognise them and take them on board before somebody else does. Work hard at it and persevere, as ideas, money or opportunities don't drop out of the sky – you have to look for them. In 2006 I was given an opportunity to write the first edition of this book by Lisa Carden from A & C Black (Bloomsbury Publishing Group). I nearly turned the offer down when I was asked as I didn't think I would be able to write a book. I don't have a degree and there's a joke with my four children, who do have degrees, that I don't know any long words! Luckily I realised I was about to turn down a great opportunity and after a lot of hard work, perseverance and encouragement from Lisa it was published in 2007. I have been able to promote the book at networking events and I have always got copies of the book to sell to customers at my hotel. All in all it is a great way of raising your companies profile to customers, suppliers and staff. It has become the staff's handbook at The Cloud Hotel and all members of staff are presented with a copy of my book when they are employed to try to ensure they practice what I preach.

I am reminded of the story of the two girls who were walking along the street when they came across a pond. They heard voices coming from the pond and when they looked down there were two frogs shouting 'Get us out, get us out'. The first girl put her hands together and the frog jumped out and landed in her hands. 'What do you want me to do now?' asked the girl. The frog replied: 'Give me a kiss, and I'll turn into a handsome young man'. So the girl gave him a kiss and a handsome young man appeared! The second girl put her hands together and the other frog jumped out of the pond but just as he was about to land the girl opened her handbag and trapped the frog inside. 'What have you done that for?', the frog shouted. The girl replied, 'Handsome young men are two a penny but a talking frog is hard to come by!'

Creating the right surroundings

For any business, having attractive surroundings for both customers and staff gives everyone that feel-good factor. It doesn't have to break the bank, either. Think how much nicer it is to sit in a dentist's waiting room that is clean, with bright and cheerful décor, comfortable chairs and a smiling receptionist. A few interesting pictures on the wall, some up-to-date magazines and a vase of fresh flowers all help too. No one looks forward to going to the dentist – many people positively dread it – but waiting in pleasant surroundings helps to calm the nerves.

I know of a dentist who left the practice she was working in because the other partners would not adopt her new ideas for making the waiting room a more pleasant area for the patients (their customers) to sit in. They did not think it was important for the success of the practice, as they were all excellent dentists. She has now set up her own business in beautiful surroundings where her patients are able to relax and enjoy their visits. The result? Her turnover has trebled!

Again, remember that first impressions always count. One of the most important areas of any business is the outside of the building and it is often overlooked. You need to attract new customers into your business and if the outside of the building has been neglected and is shabby what impression does that give to a prospective customer? When customers walk into your establishment, whether it is a garage, hotel, butcher's shop or travel agency, they'll form an opinion of your business within the first five seconds. So think about what you can do to get them on board! For example:

- Hotels and restaurants will be judged first by the outside of the building, then by their lobby and reception area. You could have colourful, well-kept-gardens and hanging baskets, as well as having an attractive arrangement of fresh flowers at the entrance of the hotel to welcome customers. This should go without saying but I will remind you – make sure that everywhere is spotlessly clean, well painted and free of dust.

- If your customers need to wait, for instance if you run a garage where people have to wait while an MOT is done on their car, make sure they have somewhere to sit. Comfortable chairs and the offer of a cup of tea or coffee will work wonders.

- If you run a hair salon, say, and you have a lot of senior clients, think about how you can make them comfortable as they wait for their appointment. Modern chairs may look attractive but are not always comfortable. I recently invested in a few armchairs that are slightly raised to accommodate my more senior customers. I had noticed how much difficulty they were having in getting out of chairs of an average height, so I tailored my purchase to their needs. This small investment has delighted them, but of course these chairs would not be appropriate for a wine bar where the customers are probably a lot younger. Again, it's question of identifying what your market wants.

- If you create your products on-site, let customers see what you do. It's a great way to get them involved and also, if you work in the food industry, they can make a note of your high standards of hygiene. Kerry Kirchin, who runs Cakes by Kerry in Widnes, Cheshire (www.cakesbykerry.com) bakes celebration cakes for weddings, birthdays, anniversaries and so on. Kerry designed her shop so that customers can see her kitchen, get a sense of what she does and also smell her wonderful baking! So, for instance, if you make and sell your own pottery, you could let customers see where your pots are baked and glazed.

Recently I was in London to meet a group of friends for lunch. We had reserved a table at a West End hotel but when we arrived the chairs were so uncomfortable, the air conditioning had made the restaurant so cold and the lighting was so dark that we left and found somewhere else to eat. The restaurant was empty and I imagine it will stay that way until the owners recognise that serving good food is not the only thing that will keep customers happy — surroundings need to be comfortable and welcoming. I wonder if the owners of such establishments ever experience their services as a customer. The impression I came away with was that this company had more money than sense and was more concerned with creating a showroom instead of a profitable business!

Looking after your staff

Your staff will respond to comfortable, attractive and safe surroundings just as much as your customers will. Of course, the nature of the building you're based in, or the industry in which you operate, may limit your choices, but you should do your absolute best to provide excellent conditions for your staff as well as providing them with the right equipment that is not only efficient but also safe. Make sure that the 'back-stage area' (as I call it) is safe, clean and bright. A dull, dreary environment does not encourage your staff to perform to the high standards you expect from them.

Again, this won't be appropriate for every industry, but having a uniform for the staff makes them look smart and ensures they don't turn up to work in unsuitable clothing. Remember, they are representing you and your business. Often in small businesses the staff have no guidance as to how they should dress for work and they appear untidy and unkempt. This doesn't portray a good image for the company. Having a uniform that your staff find attractive to wear and is comfortable raises their self-esteem and again helps create that feel-good factor. It should, of course, be practical as well as eye-catching and relevant to the sector you are working in but there is no reason why it can't also be fashionable. I change our hotel uniform every few years to continue to present a fresh, up-to-date image. I try to choose a uniform that is smart and modern as well as practical for my business. A member of staff who wears their uniform with pride and confidence is more likely to give excellent service and create a good impression and drive success.

The cost and the care of the uniforms have to be controlled but to me it is a worthwhile investment. It is not necessary to spend a lot of money for them to be comfortable and presentable, bearing in mind that you will probably be changing them every so often and therefore they don't have to last for years. I always consult my staff when making the final choice about the uniform, as this makes them feel involved and ensures they will be happy with the result, after all it is your staff who will be wearing it. It is a team effort and we use our imagination to try and choose a uniform that will be noticed and stand out from our competitors'. Having a smart uniform projects a strong and professional company.

I'm often asked who manages the hotel when I'm not there. The answer I give is 'my team'. I have created a self-managed team where each department takes responsibility for its own specific area. Everyone should take time away from their business and be able to delegate to their staff and trust that the business will still be there when you get back. I encourage my staff to develop their leadership skills and work together to make things happen. In a small business, you don't need to have expensive layers of management to maintain momentum. To keep my staff motivated, I like to put posters with a message on the walls (for example, 'If you don't look after the customer, someone else will'). These posters have to be changed regularly to keep the interest of the staff. After a while they will become part of the everyday furnishings, and not make any impact so you need to change them regularly to create an interest and keep the staff motivated.

Be imaginative

The suggestions I have touched on so far have all been visual as that is what most people remember and notice first. That is why it is paramount for a shop to have an eye-catching window display that seduces the customers and tempts them into the shop. It doesn't have to be elaborate – in fact, it can be quite simple – but it needs to stand out from the strong competition that all retailers are facing not only with their immediate rivals but also with so many Internet sites nowadays.

How often do you find yourself browsing in a shopping centre, with no definite intention of buying anything, when an imaginative window display catches your eye? You are drawn into the shop to look at the products in more detail and, before you know it, you've bought something! It's all down to clever and creative marketing. It's essential that retailers are innovative and use their imagination if they want to see increased sales and higher profitability.

A small, privately owned gift shop in my local area is well known for its eye-catching window displays. They are always themed and represent different events that are happening throughout the year or the seasons. I know the owner well and am aware that his window displays are done on a tight budget, although the final effect is brilliant. Most people can't pass the shop without going in to browse and invariably end up buying something. The result: a very successful business.

I'm fortunate enough to be able to benefit from this business owner's talent every year at Christmas, when he looks after the festive decorations at The Cloud. The design changes annually, is unique to us and has become our trademark at Christmas time. Our customers often ask us when the decorations will be going up so that they can come and see them. In fact, I have often considered having a 'turning on the lights' celebration as they do on many major high streets, but maybe that is a little over the top!

I was returning from a business trip to Switzerland with the gift-shop owner. It was February and the weather had been absolutely wonderful while we were there, with blue skies and mild temperatures. Of course, the mild weather and lack of snow had affected the tourist trade in Switzerland badly and we were discussing the consequences of global warming on our return journey. With my hotelier hat on, I was saying that warmer summers might persuade the British people to take their holidays at home and that the tourist business would benefit from the change in climate.

My friend pointed out to me that the warm weather is not so beneficial to retailers such as him who sell gifts and luxury commodities, as potential customers would rather be out in the fresh air or on the beach than shopping. For example, he has previously done a roaring trade in small chocolate gifts and 'favours' for weddings and other special events, and of course people are reluctant to buy chocolate in hot weather. Realising that he had to change his selling tactics, my friend decided to concentrate on selling merchandise for the garden and outside activities for the summer season. He will now be offering decorative tablecloths, table clips and picnic products as well as garden ornaments. He has recognised just how quickly his market can change and shown that you can survive by being alert to that change, acting quickly and reinventing your product.

His shop also offers a gift-wrapping service at no extra cost to the customer and a very small cost to his business. It's just a sheet of wrapping paper and some ribbon, but it saves the customer time and increases the 'wow' factor to the present's recipient. The customer will then tell other friends and family members about the service. Adding value for the customer in this way, in turn, produces an increase in customer numbers and positive financial rewards.

Make sure your words pack a punch

Your adverts, brochures, websites, business cards and logos do a lot of the legwork when it comes to promoting your business. They provide the information about your company that consumers are searching for. It is very easy to get carried away with the idea of advertising, but spending a fortune on it probably is not the best use of available cash for a small business.

Many businesses are bombarded with phone calls trying to persuade them to advertise in magazines, newspapers and at charity events. It often takes trial and error to discover which advertising is working for you and where you are getting the positive response and sales. Unless you monitor the response very closely you could find you are throwing money down the drain. From my experience I have found a few lines in a national newspaper to include your website and phone number can bring in a good response and also be cost effective. So whenever you get a phone or Internet query, always ask customers where they heard of you: it's a very simple test to discover which advertising is producing results and bringing increased business, which is the whole Idea of advertising.

Although your adverts need to be creative and eye catching they don't need to be too long or too expensive. The following punning advert caught my eye for a firm of optometrists when I was in South Africa:

A man with vision

Simple but creative!

Spreading the word online

It is easy to get your message across to the public in just a few powerful words. The idea is to make them hungry for more information about your product. They can find that on your website, as long as you remember to include your website address in your advert.

Why is it important to have a website? Well, your website is like a shop window. It's an electronic brochure that advertises your business or organisation all day, every day, to potential customers from all over the world. To get the most from your website, make sure it is:

- well designed
- informative
- easy to read
- kept up to date! There's nothing worse than visiting a site only to find that it was last updated five years ago, and so bears no relation to your needs
- most businesses these days have a blog, Facebook, Twitter and sometimes YouTube on their website. Select the media that is suitable for your business as you don't always need them all, just because everyone else has them.

It's relatively easy to create your own website if you have the technical expertise, but if you'd rather get professional help, engage the services of a website designer. Ask for recommendations from friends, colleagues or networking contacts before you hire someone. It's a good idea to invite maybe two or three potential designers for a chat before you make your final decision. This ensures that:

- they will know more about you and your business
- you can explain exactly what you want and why – give them as much information as you can about your likely customers and what they might be looking for. If you know that some of your customers have disabilities, such as visual impairment, ask the designer to make sure the website is accessible to everyone (the Web Accessibility Initiative's site has some useful background information on this at www. w3.org/WAI/gettingstarted/Overview.html)
- you can both tell whether you'd be able to work together successfully
- they can show you some of their previous work online

This is also the time to discuss the budget. Be very clear about what your shoestring funds can stretch to, and make sure that, as with any estimate, the designer has included all relevant costs. You don't want any nasty surprises later.

Whether you put the site together yourself or get some outside help, remember to include:

'About us'. This section doesn't have to be very long, but it should contain a brief section about you and your business and what you're setting out to do. Your elevator pitch will come in handy here! For example, if you supply Fairtrade products, explain why or what prompted you to start trading this way. If you only use the freshest ingredients from within a 20-mile radius of your shop, tell the customer. Explain the benefits of what your business does in a concise (see below) and entertaining way.

Contact details. Whether you want people to buy from your site or pop into your shop, don't forget to let them know how they can get in touch if they have a question or don't know where you're based. In this section, list your phone number, contact e-mail address, physical address with a map if possible and opening hours too (if appropriate).

Information about your products and services. Now is the time to tell people exactly what your business supplies. What you say will depend very much on what you're selling of course, but try to keep it brief yet informative so that people don't 'switch off'. Think carefully about what you would want to know if you were a potential customer. For example:

- If you were looking for a room in a hotel or B&B, you'd want to know the price, the type and sizes of rooms available, the location, what's on in the area and places of interest to visit.
- If you wanted to buy a new exhaust pipe for your car, you'd want to know the labour costs, what guarantees are offered and so on.
- If you wanted to buy only free-range, organic meat, you'd want to know that the food was completely traceable.

Prices. Some businesses seem to be reluctant to feature prices online. This is understandable if, say, they make bespoke furniture and prices depend on exactly what the customer needs to fit in that difficult space in the lounge, but I do believe that ballpark figures at least should be shown. You're trying to encourage customers to buy and trust you, remember, not drive them mad with frustration. If you run a restaurant, café, hotel or bar, make sure that any room rates or meal offers are accurate and that you're very clear about what customers will be getting for their money. Nothing irritates a customer more than finding out they have to pay more for your services or products than originally quoted. Don't offer them one thing online and then add on lots of extras when they come to pay the bill or they won't be coming back.

Illustrations. Most websites benefit from some photos or carefully chosen illustrations, as long as they're good quality and there are not too many of them. Websites with too many images can take a long time to download, and you don't want to put people off by getting bored! If you use photos on your site (as we do on The Cloud's website), make sure they are of a high enough resolution to be viewed clearly and keep them up to date, changing them regularly if necessary.

Carewords

Another way of spreading the word about your business online is by selecting the right wording to put on your site. In his book *Killer Web Content* (Bloomsbury, 2006), Internet content specialist Gerry McGovern explains that to make your website a success, the content on it should feature 'carewords': these are the words customers are looking for as they try to buy or find out about something, and they are a call to action. Think carefully about what your customers will be looking for on your site, and then write (or brief someone else to write) the content to fit that. If you put the customer first, you won't go far wrong.

Visual impact

When you mention the word 'creative', everyone immediately thinks about the artistic side of business, anything visual — furnishings, décor, artwork, flowers and so on. The written word is just as important and plays an essential role in creating the right impression of your company and conveying clear messages. To capitalise on that, aim to achieve the same high standards for all your printed materials as you would for your other products and services.

- Check the website for spelling and grammatical errors. Bloomsbury's *Good Word Guide* and *Good Grammar Guide* are a boon here. If you're not confident about your grammatical skills or knowledge, ask a trusted friend or colleague to help.
- Don't let your standards drop when you write business e-mails. Make sure that you've spelled your correspondent's name correctly (don't call her 'Liz' if her name is 'Lisa', for example) and that you sign off politely. If you get a complaint or an angry e-mail from someone (see Chapter 9), it's very tempting to write back in kind, but don't do it! Never reply to an e-mail in anger (you don't know who it could be sent on to): if you're furious, go away and do something else for half an hour, and reply when you've calmed down. The same goes for responding to letters, although I usually leave

it for a day before I reply to allow me to calm down, especially if I feel the complaint isn't reasonable and not all customer complaints are.

■ Make sure your letters are well laid out and easy to read, bearing in mind the age of the person you are writing to if you know it. Older customers often need large and clear text.

Creative 'scripts'

This sounds a little contradictory, doesn't it? Have you ever called a business and had the phone answered by someone who sounds as if they've just got out of bed and are totally disinterested in your call? Did you call them back? I would be most surprised if you did.

Not long ago, I had to make a telephone enquiry about a sensitive and important planning application. The girl who answered the phone had the dreariest voice and droned on unhelpfully. (So much so, I wondered whether I was talking to a robot.) I was in a cheeky mood that day and mirrored her voice and attitude and I don't think she even noticed.

To avoid this happening in your business, make sure that all the staff who answer the phone to customers have been trained: the costs will be minimal in comparison to the rewards. Whether it is a private or public company is irrelevant: the response and the way the phone is answered should always be upbeat, positive and friendly. First impressions are important and can determine whether a potential customer decides to do business with you. We try to respond to e-mail enquiries by phone if possible as we believe this way we are able to have better contact with the customer and communicate with them on a more personal level. By speaking to them personally it enables us to give the customer more information about the hotel and an opportunity to answer their questions and find out their requirements promptly. I think it gives us a better chance of getting a sale.

Encourage your staff to use their imagination when answering the phone or speaking to your customers. Let them be themselves and create their own script, so long as it is suitable for your organisation.

If you are starting a new business, give careful attention to the name of the company. It needs to be short and punchy, and a name that people will remember. Make it unusual and even a little off-beat if appropriate. If you already run your own business, maybe think of changing the company name if it's not catchy enough. Use your imagination: perhaps set up a competition among your staff to see who can think of the most suitable and innovative name. The name of your company can provide a good talking point with your customers.

Customers are always interested to know how The Cloud Hotel acquired its name. The story goes like this. It was originally four small cottages, built in 1900. One of the owners had bought his cottage with his winnings from the St Cloud racecourse in France. When the cottages were converted into a hotel, it became The St Cloud Hotel, and I have a photo of the hotel at that time. I have no idea when the 'St' was dropped, but I always joke with the customers that it was when I came to the hotel. Try to think of a name for your business that creates interest and is easy to remember.

DELIGHTING YOUR CUSTOMERS

Every day I try to think of new ways to do things at The Cloud so that we stand out from the crowd. It can be easier than you think to delight your customers on a shoestring, and small details can make a big impact. For instance, if we have a honeymoon couple staying at the hotel we scatter rose petals on the bed. It's so simple but gives so much pleasure. Think of something different you can offer in your business to give your customers an unforgettable experience and make them want to do business with you again.

6 ASKING FOR FEEDBACK ... AND ACTING ON IT

Your customers are your future. They drive your business forward and present you with opportunities that can help your business grow. To succeed, you need to listen to them. It's essential to communicate with them in a friendly and courteous manner and build up good, honest relationships that allow them to give you feedback on your business's performance.

Once you've received feedback from your customers via questionnaires, e-mails, letters or other means, don't let all that useful information gather dust. Read it and act on it so that you can sort out any blips or further capitalise on a success.

Be flexible

There are a number of ways you can get feedback on your business. The more opportunities you have to discover how people feel about your products and services, the better chance you have of becoming excellent at what you do. Even if the feedback you get makes painful reading at times, it's incredibly valuable and you should take the opportunity to learn from negative feedback, so don't dismiss it.

Some of the most popular methods of asking for, and receiving, feedback include:

1. direct dialogue with your customers
2. written surveys and questionnaires
3. visitors' books and comment cards
4. the Internet, blogging and e-mail
5. friends and family
6. members of staff and suppliers
7. letters
8. bank manager
9. Facebook, Twitter and blogs
10. official inspectors and mystery shoppers
11. Tripadvisor for the hospitality and leisure industry

Direct dialogue

Talk to your customers! Throughout this book I've stressed how important it is to communicate with your customers, make them feel special and find out what they expect from you. Anyone who wants to buy from you has the potential to become a valuable, long-standing customer. They will have their own opinion of your service and products, so it's to your advantage if you know what that opinion is so that you can increase the value of your relationship.

Customers at The Cloud often give me excellent suggestions on ways to improve the facilities and services in the hotel. Sometimes an idea appears so obvious that I can't believe I hadn't thought of it myself, but that's the advantage of customers seeing your business through a different lens. If you've started your business from scratch, you get so embroiled in the minutiae at times that it can be very difficult to stand back and view the company objectively.

Your customers are thankfully free of the horrors of paperwork, finances, and staffing issues and can give you that perspective. Listen to them and the small changes they mention could not only make them more likely to come back, but also help you lift your game overall. It can be something as simple as adjusting the layout of a bedroom in a hotel, or changing the way information is presented on your website, or even recommending a member of staff for promotion.

Some larger organisations have dedicated feedback or customer services telephone numbers that you can call. I was in South Africa on holiday recently and noticed that on the label of a bottle of their mineral water, Nestlé had printed 'Talk to us' with a free phone number for customers to use. It went on to say 'It's good to know'. It was as simple as that, but nevertheless a powerful message.

Written surveys and questionnaires

Some people just aren't very good at talking to others and find it hard to express their feelings to you directly. They may be shy and reserved, or just too embarrassed to tell you exactly what they think of your services. Their views are still very helpful, though, so do create a feedback mechanism that will suit them. Written surveys and questionnaires could fit the bill. Make sure they are:

- **relevant to your particular industry**
- **short**
- **easy to complete**

If a survey is too long and the questions too complex, it will take an age to complete and most people just won't bother. I know I certainly won't as I'm so busy running my own business. Usually, the same question appears several times over, with the wording tweaked slightly in places. I've read surveys where I can't even understand the questions, let alone answer them! Keep the questions simple and easy enough for the average person to complete, and a much higher percentage of customers will give you feedback and, ultimately, valuable criticism and opportunities.

It can be frustrating to have customers who, when asked if everything is to their satisfaction, assure you that it is and then send you a letter of complaint a few days later. Maybe they were too embarrassed to tell you to your face that they were unhappy with something, but you would at least have had the chance to correct the mistake there and then. It's the same as customers who eat all their food and then complain that the meat was tough! If they'd told us earlier, we could have offered them an alternative. As a business you need honest feedback from your customers and not everyone is very good at giving this. These are what I call the silent customers but they will have plenty to say about you to their friends and colleagues. Be wary of them as they can do untold damage to your business without you knowing!

Incentives

Whatever feedback mechanism you use, one way to encourage people to reply is to offer an incentive. Don't worry, you don't need to spend a fortune: you could offer a free bottle of wine, book, sandwich, manicure, coffee and cake, a short-run leaflet printing, according to the nature of your business.

Visitors' books and comment cards

Visitors' books and comment cards can now be found on shop counters, in hotel reception areas and in many other places. They are a valuable and cost-effective way of collecting your customers' comments and advice. At The Cloud, we have a visitors' book placed strategically at reception and we always make sure there is a pen to hand to encourage guests to write their comments in the book before they leave. (Having to rummage about for a pen is an extra obstacle.)

Make sure every member of your staff gets the chance to read the remarks and reflect on them. My 'back-stage team' — the chefs, kitchen porters, maintenance team — obviously don't spend a lot of time in the reception area and wouldn't see the comments if I didn't make sure they all had the opportunity to read them too. Involving the whole team is a crucial part of increasing morale, celebrating great performance and mulling over areas that can be improved. It gives the staff food for thought, raises their self-esteem, makes them feel valued and often sparks off new ideas.

The Internet, blogging and e-mail

If your business has a website (and most businesses should have in this age of technology), it can take customers just a few minutes to get in touch and let you know how you're doing. You can install a simple form that can be filled in, or dedicate a special e-mail address for comments. For example, Innocent Drinks, who produce smoothies and fruit juices, can be contacted at hello@innocentdrinks.co.uk; Liz Earle skincare at naturallyactive@lizearle.com. You get the picture!

A business blog can be an effective promotion tool and allows a company to reach new audiences via its website. It gives your company and your staff a place to collect and share ideas and information with your customers. It also puts a 'face' to your business, which can be a great help if you yourself don't have a lot of personal contact with customers (for instance if you run a mail-order business or a road- haulage company).

Your website will probably always be customers' first port of call if they want to find out more about your company, check out any special offers and so on, but a blog gives you the opportunity to expand on the information on your website and give it a more personal feel. It is an effective way of communicating with millions of people but it must be updated regularly for it to be effective. For more information about blogging, read our sister publication *Making an impact online . . . on a Shoestring* by Antóin Ó Lachtnáin.

Family and friends

My family can be very honest in their criticism and often come up with ideas, so it's always worth inviting your own family to give you their feedback. They obviously have your best interests at heart and (generally!) want to see you succeed.

Of course, if members of your family are involved with the running of the business, you'll automatically hear their points of view and this can sometimes cause conflict. My children were brought up in the business and therefore have an insight about how the hotel should operate. When they visit me now, they experience the hotel as any other customers would, and they're able to evaluate their experience more objectively and give me constructive feedback as a result which I always welcome even if sometimes I don't agree with them!

My friends have also given me feedback, although they tend to be more polite and are not as frank as my family! Nevertheless, every piece of information you receive is valuable in helping you find out how your customers feel about your business. No information is ever wasted so long as you are a good listener and open to suggestions.

It is surprising how everyone thinks they are an expert in your business and, although they mean well, some of their suggestions are just neither possible nor practical so you have to be diplomatic and somehow think of how to decline their suggestion politely without offending them.

Members of staff and suppliers

A business that understands the importance of communicating with both its external and internal customers is more likely to receive and benefit from constructive feedback. An 'open-door' culture, where staff feel at ease with the management and their fellow workers, and are not afraid to air their views and share information with each other, is the sign of a happy and healthy establishment. It's not just how customers feel about your business that can make or break it; it's important to know how your employees feel and whether they enjoy their work. Your staff will only treat your customers as well as they are being treated, and they must come first. Remember, happy and motivated staff means happy customers, and happy customers result in a healthy balance sheet.

If your staff are frustrated or are having issues regarding a difficult customer, a colleague, the way things are done, or perhaps their pay (always a very sensitive subject), it is essential that they feel able to approach you so that you can discuss their concerns. Weekly meetings are the ideal way of keeping in touch with your staff, but these may not be possible or practical for every business, particularly if your business operates on shifts.

At The Cloud, we're operational 24/7 and there's never a time — except when all the customers are asleep — when one of us isn't required to perform some duty or other, and the phone never stops ringing. It's very rare that I can gather the whole team together at any one time and our staff meetings can become very disjointed.

To combat this, I hold regular five-minute meetings with the different departments at a convenient time that suits everyone. This means that I can pass on any relevant information to my staff and ask them for their comments, too. I try to keep my own contribution to a minimum so that everyone else has the chance to participate actively and get their message across to me and to the rest of the team. These meetings also give me an opportunity to thank them for a job well done and pass on any compliments I have received from guests about a particular member of staff's excellent service and attitude. I have also introduced a staff monthly newsletter which gives me another opportunity to thank them for their loyalty and hard work. It also gives me a chance to address issues I am not happy about and to constantly remind them of the high standards I expect from them. Whatever business you are in training is ongoing and you have to constantly remind staff that the customer is king. I always start and end my newsletters with a positive message.

When you're running a business, it often feels as if you spend your life dashing about solving the next big issue that raises its head. Of course, you have to keep on top of things, but do take time to praise your staff and also pass on any feedback that they can learn from. Be careful about the way you phrase it, so that (even if feedback has been poor) your staff know what you want and what you expect them to do about it – be specific. Passing on good feedback can have an incredibly positive and energising effect on the whole team and motivate them into making further improvements in their work and performance.

These five-minute meetings at The Cloud often demonstrate to me the enthusiasm of my staff and how passionate they are about finding new ways of improving our customer service. I make sure that the atmosphere is relaxed (with the added bonus of tea and biscuits!) to put everyone at their ease. All this helps the team to bond and it breaks down any barriers.

My policy is that everyone who has any contact with the hotel is a potential customer. Luckily, The Cloud has a large audience and there are many opportunities to attract visitors who come for a holiday, a short break or just for a meal out. We treat our suppliers, advertisers, accountant and even the dreaded inspectors with the same friendly attitude and respect with which we treat our guests. All these people will form an impression of the hotel based on the reception they receive from us, and they will pass on their opinion to their friends and family as well as to their other customers — our suppliers' delivery men are always keen to let us know how busy our competitor hotels and restaurants are and we are always interested to know! We enjoy and absorb any information they can give us about our competitors and learn from their comments.

One spin-off benefit of having a good relationship with your suppliers is that once they get to know you and your business, they'll keep you posted about any special offers their companies are launching and which may be of interest to you. This sometimes gives you an advantage over your competitors, and some potential savings to boot. It's a two-way process: you swap feedback and hopefully you'll both win and profit from the relationship.

Letters

Yes, some people still write them! Nothing gives me greater pleasure than receiving a letter thanking the staff and myself for excellent service and an enjoyable experience at The Cloud. Every single member of the team appreciates this, too. It builds confidence and lifts our spirits, helping to create that all-important feel-good factor.

I always pin these letters on the staff noticeboard for everyone to see and enjoy. I make a point of acknowledging every letter I receive, not just to let the customer know that I have received it, but also to thank them for taking the trouble to write in the first place.

Of course, every business receives letters of complaint from time to time and The Cloud is no exception. No one wants an unhappy customer, but we all make mistakes, and so long as you get it right most of the time, and learn from your mistakes, you will succeed. Obviously, I wish we didn't have any complaints, but they have to be dealt with and, while you may not agree with all the negative comments, there will probably be one or two in which you can recognise a kernel of truth. Act on these and tell your correspondent what you're going to do about them. Also, alert your staff to what has happened so that they're aware of the issue and don't repeat the error.

The bank manager!

Although even the thought of bank managers can make some small-business owners feel panicky, they're a useful resource. They give you feedback on your financial situation and will usually offer constructive advice and help.

Let's say you have a business idea that you'd like to explore, but you only have a limited budget. You would probably go to your bank manager first to present your idea, ask for his or her opinion and find out whether he or she would be prepared to support you in your new venture. Ultimately, you're asking for feedback on your proposal in the hope that the bank will lend you the money you require.

Many businesses rely on their banks to keep them afloat and trading. In this instance it's best to work very closely with your bank manager and keep him or her informed of your financial position, ideally on a weekly basis.

When I was first widowed and The Cloud was in dire financial straits, I had to send monthly financial reports to my bank manager outlining the current situation as well as my financial forecast for the following month. This enabled him to give me appropriate advice and also protected the bank's interest. I certainly would not still be in business if it weren't for him: he supported me through thick and thin and has seen me come out of a long black tunnel with a successful, healthy business.

Always keep in touch with your bank manager. Inform him or her of any financial difficulties and don't bury your head in the sand. Bank managers will sympathise with your problems *so long as* you tell them what's happening. Let them know if you can predict some good sales and when you expect these to materialise. Most disagreements between bank manager and client are down to a lack of communication.

Official inspectors and mystery shoppers

Most businesses have to contend with inspectors at one time or another and the number and type will depend on the industry you operate in. Being in the hospitality business we have to entertain a wide variety of these individuals. They certainly are an interruption to my day as they usually arrive unannounced while I'm in the middle of my work and then expect me to stop what I'm doing to listen to their comments and advice.

Still, I've learned to greet them with open arms and listen carefully to their views, as they are seeing my business from the customer's perspective. It's very easy when you have been in a workplace for a number of years to overlook certain aspects of the business: it's not that you don't care any more, but it all becomes so familiar that you just don't always notice a carpet that is wearing out or a room that needs redecorating.

Think over all the suggestions carefully and then prioritise them. Some ideas just wouldn't be cost-effective to implement, especially if money is tight. If an inspector tells you that something must be changed for health or safety reasons, then clearly you need to tackle that right away. For all non-essential proposals, though, assess what would work most effectively for your customers: you know them best. Nevertheless, the inspectors' feedback is very valuable and it keeps me on my toes! Something I'm quite used to, having been a dancer!

I've never actually employed a mystery shopper to scrutinise my hotel as I get most feedback for free from our customers and other people I meet, sometimes in the most unexpected places. I don't want to spend my income on what I consider to be an unnecessary service. It's a question of being alert to information that is fed to you, whether at a dinner party, a social event or even chatting to someone on a train or plane. Having said that, mystery shoppers may be useful in other industries, especially the retail sector.

Keep your ears and eyes open for new ideas that crop up: they don't all occur in business meetings or other formal occasions. Often when people are relaxed and having fun, they have fewer inhibitions and may disclose useful information. It's then up to you to identify the opportunities that have been presented to you: decide which ones you are going to implement, and then do it! You have two ears, two eyes and one mouth – use them in that order and you will be amazed at what you learn.

Brainstorming

So what do you do with all the feedback you gather, from all of these potential sources? Well, first of all you have to decide if the ideas are relevant to – and realistic for – your type of business. Brainstorming is a great way to talk over ideas with your team, taking input from everyone so that you can all 'buy in' to any new strategies you come up with. To get the best from a brainstorming session:

1. Focus on what you want to achieve

Do you want to increase the number of customers you have? Reduce the number of complaints you're getting? Expand your range of products and services? Work out what you're aiming for so that you can set some parameters. If you turn up to the session saying that you want to 'just make everything better', how would you know where to start?

2. Decide who should be there

Obviously you have to be there, and if your business is small enough you could ask every single member of the team to be present, too. It may be worth inviting some trusted friends, colleagues or advisors, though, to give you a more objective view of the ideas you'll be discussing. If your business has grown to the extent that you have a team of managers in place, you might want to limit the meeting to just them but ask each one to talk to his or her respective staff members beforehand so that any insightful ideas or comments can be included in your discussions.

3. Pick a sensible time

If the busiest time of the week for you is 12pm on Friday, it wouldn't make much sense to arrange the meeting for then! Set aside an hour or so early in the day and stick to that. If someone has to man the phones or e-mail, ask that person for any contributions beforehand so that they feel involved. Then, the next time you hold a meeting, make sure that someone else takes a turn at holding the fort.

4. Find a good venue

Ideally, you need a light, bright room that can comfortably accommodate all attendees. Ask everyone to turn their mobile phones off before the meeting starts.

5. Appoint a 'moderator'

This is where one of your outside colleagues or advisors could be particularly useful. Ask them to make a note of all the ideas that arise during the initial phase of the meeting. A big white board or flipchart can be useful for this.

6. Don't rule anything out!

When you ask all the attendees for their views on how you can make improvements, make a note of everything suggested, even if it sounds too wacky to work – some *element* of it might be just what is required.

7. Take a break

If people are running out of steam, take a break. Ask them to come up with (say) five more ideas before they head off for a coffee!

8. Go back and refine your list

After the break, go back and look at your main list, this time scrutinising each suggestion carefully. How cost-effective is it? Is it realistic? What would be the measurable benefits to your business? Be rigorous and reject anything that wouldn't have a significant, positive impact on your bottom line.

9. Make it happen!

Once you've whittled down the list and identified the most realistic options, it would be a great waste of your time and energy if you didn't commit to putting those great ideas into practice. Obviously, you don't have to do them all at once, but set yourself (or your managers) a deadline and stick to it, otherwise it is easy to forget as you get bogged down once again with running the business. Monitor the progress so that you can check that the new ideas are yielding good results. If they don't (and some won't – that's to be expected), stop doing it. Don't tie up any more resources in them and move on.

10. Keep your team up to date

Put an update on your noticeboard, send an e-mail or simply take a few minutes at your next staff meeting to tell everyone what happened at the meeting (if they didn't go), and how the new initiatives are progressing. Praise the person or people who came up with the initiatives (if it wasn't you) so that they know their contribution has been appreciated.

Be bold enough to try out this process and see what comes out of it. As business management guru Peter Drucker noted: 'Wherever you see a successful business, someone has made a courageous decision.' There is no doubt that life in a small business can be tough, but there are some advantages: you can react quickly to new ideas without having to battle the bureaucracy that larger firms have to contend with, so make the most of it!

7 LEARNING FROM YOUR COMPETITORS

Anyone who is in business wants to be successful — otherwise there's no point in getting up every day to go to work. But to achieve that success you must be constantly seeking to improve your performance, your service and your productivity. We all want to be the very best at what we do. And that's the bottom line!

As small-business owners, we're all competing for the same customers and it can be tough out there. Customers are very discerning these days and they're not just looking for value for money, but exceptional services and products. They are the ultimate arbiters: they make the final choice as to whether to give their custom to you or to one of your competitors. To make that choice, they're looking for a unique experience that will excite them.

A few years ago, I was a judge for a women's business award. I asked one of the finalists who she thought her competitors were. Her reply was: 'I don't have any!' She was convinced that she was absolutely the best at what she did. It's great to have that level of confidence, but maybe a little naïve to believe that there really was no one out there who could have grabbed her customers. Business is a tough world and the only sensible thing to do is to keep an eye on your competitors — their successes, failures and progress. There may be a lot you can learn from them in the process.

Who are your competitors?

The first step is to define who the main competitors are in your industry. Anyone in the same core business, whether a small, medium or large organisation, is a competitor and therefore a potential threat to your bottom line.

Existing businesses

As a small business, your main threat comes from organisations that offer a similar product and service in the same area, so you need to be aware of who is doing what, how and where. For example, I keep track of the small country hotels and restaurants that are a similar size to mine within a radius of 10 miles. As an accommodation provider, I also have to watch out for any bed-and-breakfast establishments that may suddenly appear and offer competitive rates. Keep an open mind and watch out for businesses that may not be exactly the same as yours, but which offer a certain level of overlap.

There is a small country house hotel a few miles from my hotel. I regard it as one of my main competitors, yet every new idea I come up with seems to appear in this hotel a few months later! This used to really irritate me until I realised that I could turn the situation to my advantage. Knowing that people are borrowing my ideas drives me to constantly be thinking of new approaches. It encourages me to implement new initiatives, stay one step ahead and be unique.

New businesses

As well as looking at what your established competitors are doing, you'd be wise to look out for any new businesses that appear. Your local newspaper is a good source of this type of information and will often trail a new business opening, especially if it's unusual or innovative in some way. Customers love trying out something new, so be prepared and find out as much as you can about the products and services they offer, as well as their prices. Until you can prove otherwise, assume your competitors are as good as you, if not better. You can never afford to relax and become complacent, as soon as you do you will find your customers will go elsewhere and your competitiors will take your business.

Asking the right questions

Word of mouth is an incredibly powerful marketing tool and it can make or break a small business, especially if many of your customers are local. Customers love to talk and exchange ideas and experiences, and if they have tried out the products and services of one of your competitors, draw on that information to determine your next steps. What did they enjoy? What didn't work so well? Be subtle and, of course, don't be seen to bad-mouth rival businesses or business owners, but do listen out for useful clues.

Your staff can also help you out on this score, in different ways. Firstly, they have direct contact with your customers and will have built up good relationships with long-standing ones. They're in an excellent position to do informal research on your behalf. Also, outside of work, your staff are customers too. My team goes out and experiences other hotels and restaurants and regularly reports back to me any good ideas they've spotted. They tell me if where they went was busy and whether the customers were enjoying themselves. They will often bring back a menu or price list for me to compare with ours so I can see where we stand in the marketplace.

The good news is that you don't have to spend a fortune on this type of research. A lot can be gleaned simply by keeping your ears and eyes open and listening to friends and colleagues. This way, I can discover if my competitors are offering value for money and what are their strong selling points, and I learn from it. I try to find out the following details about their hotels:

- **location**
- **rates**
- **access to car parking**
- **quality of service and product**
- **staff attitude to the customer**

Understanding the changes taking place in your market is crucial to retaining existing customers. I listen carefully to what other people are saying and make a note of it; even when I go on holiday, I always have a notebook to hand. In fact, my staff wait for me to produce my list when I get back as I always return with fresh ideas, anything from a new way of delivering a service to new dishes for the menus. Attention to detail is what counts and it can make all the difference to a customer's experience of staying with you. For example, I now have torches in all the bedside tables in case there is a power cut. This is an idea I picked up in a hotel I visited on holiday. My customers are delighted with such a small gesture and the cost to my business is minimal.

When you're making decisions about your business, keep your staff in the loop so that they feel engaged with the future growth of your company. It can be hard to 'let go' if you're used to being in sole control of things, but getting the perspective of others on new ideas, challenges and opportunities is extremely valuable.

Location

Having an excellent location is vital for the success of every business, but even more so for a small company. Your business needs to grab people's attention, be easily accessible, and having ample parking will usually be a big bonus, too. It's the whole experience, from travelling and parking to shopping and dining that will keep your customers coming back.

The Cloud Hotel is in the heart of the New Forest and has panoramic views of the area, but despite these great advantages the location isn't absolutely perfect. New customers sometimes have difficulty finding us as we're somewhat off the beaten track and the turning to the hotel is concealed. People often drive by and miss the turning even though there's a brown tourist sign at the end of the road directing people to us. As a result, customers may arrive tired and grumpy after having driven round in circles — we've even had to direct them via their mobile phones! Once they do arrive, it's our challenge to welcome them as if they were long-lost friends, soothe frazzled nerves and help them to relax. We are just pleased we didn't lose them to one of our competitors whom they could find more easily and might have even passed while looking for us.

Access to car parking

Unfortunately, our parking area isn't big enough to cater for the volume of business we now enjoy. The National Park will not allow us to expand and English Nature have objected because of the protected species of grass which grows in the New Forest. To cap it all, our neighbours don't welcome the additional cars, either. As the business has grown in volume and reputation over the past decade, the lack of parking has become an issue.

To counter this, I drew on something I'd noted at another hotel and decided to employ a car park attendant. I was lucky enough to find a retired gentleman to take on this task and he has now become a well-known member of staff, with great character. The cars get parked in an orderly manner and he has doubled the capacity of the car park.

The customers are delighted because they are greeted by a friendly member of staff, who helps them out of their cars. Many of my customers — particularly at lunchtime — are elderly and have some mobility problems, and he sees them safely into the hotel. Rather than being made to feel like a nuisance, they are welcomed, and my lunchtime trade has grown so much that the restaurant is full nearly every day. My customers have told me what a difference it has made to my business by having such a warm welcome, and the cost to the hotel is very small in comparison to the rewards it has reaped.

The hotel which gave me this idea was much bigger than mine, and although small businesses don't have such generous budgets as larger ones, you don't need a massive amount of money to keep customers happy: you need to give them what they want. Be creative and think carefully about what your customers would respond to best.

Offering value for money

Getting your prices right is one of the most difficult challenges for small businesses. It can be tempting, particularly if you're having cash-flow difficulties, to consistently reduce your prices so you can compete with other businesses, but don't fall into that trap. Special offers and discounts for bulk purchases are one thing, of course, but if you get into the habit of offering knock-down prices that won't cover your costs, customers will get used to it and will go elsewhere if you try to put your prices back up. A better way to have a competitive edge is by adding value to your products and services: if you run a gift shop, for example, offer to wrap presents.

However, most businesses have a lull at certain times of the year and sales drop. Competition can be fierce in these slack periods as everyone fights for the same customers, while they are all shopping around for the best deals. At these times, careful discounting can play an important role in selling your products and encourage increased sales and volume of business in off-peak periods. Take care, though, that your margins are not reduced so much that they become dangerous. With the cost of living and inflation rising it doesn't take rocket science to work out where your business will end up! For more advice on this issue, turn to Bob Gorton's book *Boosting sales ... on a Shoestring* (Bloomsbury, 2011).

Whether you're starting your business from scratch or trying to build an existing company, find out what the market will tolerate for your products and services and also what your competitors are charging. As a hotelier, I receive e-mails and mail-shots from the hotels I have stayed in over the years offering me special deals. I very seldom take them up on their offers, but these e-mails give me free information about what my competitors are charging and allow me to see where I stand in the market and what I need to do to compete.

The Internet makes this job much less of a hassle than it used to be: your competitors' websites will furnish you with most of the information you need. You can also use online comparison tools and rating sites to find out more about customers' opinions of products and services they've used, and check whether their comments apply to your business. In my line of work, the TripAdvisor site (**www.tripadvisor.co.uk**) allows users to record their experiences of hotels or restaurants anywhere in the world. Not all of the comments are positive, of course, but it can give you an overall idea of what other people are up to, what they're doing wrong ... and what they're doing right. However, do be aware that these comments are anonymous and not always genuine. Business blogs are another cost-effective way of not only marketing your business, but also learning about your competitors and customers' expectations. You must be ready to act on what you see and hear, though: it would be a waste of time to do all of that research and then not put any of the good ideas or comments into action.

Even if competitors don't have an online presence, although most do nowadays, you (or a colleague) could call them and ask for a brochure or catalogue. Also, look out for any stories or events that are trailed in your local newspaper. Is there anything you can learn from them? Whatever route you choose to do your research, do make sure that you're comparing like with like. In the leisure industry, customers can often get caught out in a restaurant or hotel when extras such as coffee, service, cover charges and VAT are unexpectedly added to the advertised price of a meal.

One of my pet hates is when VAT is added to the bill for purchased goods or services: it should be included in the quoted price. Some establishments do quote for VAT and extras, to be fair, but many don't and this disparity can confuse and annoy the customer. Similarly, in the UK, the pricing of hotels can vary enormously. Some charge for room only, others charge per person, sometimes breakfast is included, sometimes it's not. When you're researching other people's offers, do check with them if you're not sure.

This is a lesson I learned personally (albeit in a different context) when several years ago I received quotes for some construction work from three separate builders, all of whom ran small companies. Not knowing anything about building specifications at that time, which the builders recognised, in my ignorance I assumed they had all quoted for the same job. The building work coincided with a difficult period for me financially, so I gave the contract to the builder who seemed to give me the most competitive quote.

Little did I realise that this builder hadn't quoted for certain aspects of the project. The final price was almost twice as much as the original quote and nearly ruined my business. So when you're comparing prices with your competitors, be sure to research every last detail. I certainly learned from this experience and, although I have had a lot of building work done to the hotel since then, I have discovered that you only get what you pay for and if you are in any doubt it's wise to ask an expert for their advice.

The joys of networking

I am passionate about networking. Getting among your competitors and listening to what they have to say is a real eye-opener, and you'd be surprised how many people give out interesting information quite freely (especially after a few glasses of wine!). I have learned a great deal simply by attending conferences, workshops and training days – and I didn't need to spend a fortune either.

Shop around, get yourself on databases so that you're sent information about future events and then carefully select the ones that you feel would benefit you most. If you're new to networking, it's a good idea to start out with relatively low-key events before launching yourself completely: talk to the organisers of events and see if they will let you come to a meeting as a visitor (so that you can gauge how useful it really will be) before you commit to a joining fee.

Your local Chambers of Commerce should be able to give you information on networking opportunities in your area (**www. chamberonline.co.uk**). National organisations can also help. BusinessLink (**www.businesslink.gov.uk**) holds many seminars offering advice for small businesses, and these are particularly useful when you're starting up and strapped for cash – many of the seminars are free.

For women business owners, the Everywoman organisation is ideal (**www.everywoman.co.uk**): you can register your details online free of charge and you'll then receive regular newletters with useful and interesting information. Everywoman also organises regional conferences, training days and networking events where hundreds of women come together to learn, network and do business.

Listening to the speakers at events of this type is inspiring and confidence-building, so do make time to go. I don't think I've ever returned from one of these events without feeling motivated and full of new ideas to be put into action. Networking *is* work, so don't think you're wasting time. It's important for you to take time out to go to these events to meet competitors as well as potential collaborators. And don't worry, your business will still be there if you escape for a day! You'll be surprised how competent your staff can be if you're not there for them to lean on. They love the responsibility and, if something important does crop up, they can always get hold of you via your mobile phone or BlackBerry® as mobile technology has become part of everyone's life.

All the ideas I have suggested in this chapter on how to learn from your competitors add little cost to the business, but take a little time. Obviously, it's important to strike a balance between dedicating useful time to research and doing so much of it that you don't focus on your business, so use your common sense!

8 DELIVERING ON YOUR PROMISES

One of the most important ways to succeed in business is to do what you say you're going to do. That involves responding to customers' requests promptly and making sure you can deliver what you promise.

Life is about taking action. Most people, including me, find it infuriating to be kept waiting for a service or a product. I'm not talking about impatience, which often means being unreasonable. We've all experienced impatient and rude customers and have had to learn how to deal with them effectively. I'm talking about keeping your promises to your customers and making sure what you have promised them will happen . . . and happen on time.

Practise good timekeeping

Good timekeeping is a key factor in building a successful business. If none of your staff is present when your shop or office opens, how can you give your customers what they want, when they want it?

Punctuality is very important to the efficient running of any business. Explain that you'd like your staff on-site a few minutes early, not a few minutes late. Even two minutes either side of the clock can make all the difference to whether your day is productive or stressful and if you have happy or unhappy customers.

Staff who are late for work are letting their team down. As I always explain to my staff, when I was a professional dancer, being just 30 seconds late for a show meant I would have missed the opening number. It was unheard of to be late for work, and stage managers were not interested in excuses — they just expected you to be on time. Likewise, your customers are certainly not interested in your problems and why you are late for work: they have problems of their own and just want good, efficient service.

Keep in touch with customers and suppliers

Delivery times and schedules are a nightmare for business owners and customers alike. Let's say you place an order for a new piece of furniture, and you're promised that it will be delivered in six weeks. Eight weeks later, your goods haven't been delivered and because you haven't heard from the shop, you have to call them to find out what has happened to your order. You'll probably be told there has been a delay in production or some such excuse. That may be true, but your confidence in the company has been damaged because it didn't keep you up to speed with what was happening — how much can they value your order if you have to initiate all the conversations?

As ever, when dealing with customers, put yourself in their shoes and give them the service you would expect.

- **When people place an order, be realistic. Check every detail about the manufacture and delivery of a product or service *before* you give the customer a final date.**
- **Build in some slack, if you think it's appropriate. Sometimes it can be useful to build some extra time into a schedule so that if goods arrive early, your customers will be pleased at your reliability and quick**

turnaround times. The companies that deliver an order more quickly than their competitors will win more customers, and that extra business will undoubtedly increase the bottom line.

- If you think you will lose the deal and sale with the customer by being honest about the delivery time, learn to negotiate with them to achieve the desired outcome.

- Keep track of orders. Stay in touch with your suppliers and make contact regularly so that you can be kept informed of any hitches. You can then tell your customers, apologise for the delay and explain what's going on.

Get in first!

Another way of winning business and new customers ahead of your competitors (and this is a policy I'm passionate about) is to be first with the information that the customer has requested. Speed of service is what everyone is looking for these days, so take the opportunity to out-do your competitors and deliver your information more quickly and smarter than they do.

When we have an enquiry at the hotel for a brochure and tariff (yes people still do request a brochure), we know that we're likely to be one of several hotels that the customer has contacted. People ask for a brochure because they are planning a holiday or maybe a party in the restaurant, so they'll be shopping around to find the venue that most appeals to them.

My policy at The Cloud is to get every brochure that has been requested into the post *that same day*. I know we have won a lot of new customers and increased business by being so prompt and by getting there first. A member of staff is sent to catch the last collection at the post-box every day and in all weathers! You'd be wise to do the same, and any time it seems like a chore, again put yourself in your customers' position: wouldn't you be pleased and impressed if you got information promptly? It gives the impression of a well-organised business that can keep its promises – and who wouldn't want to work with a company like that?

You can, of course, put the key information about your business online these days, which saves time and money, but for items such as estimates (where prices will be very specific and based on the individual job), it's important to follow up promptly with a quote in the post. It's also sometimes a good idea to keep some information back: it's much easier to close a sale in person, when you can chat to a customer, form a relationship and convey your enthusiasm for what you're selling, than it is online.

Responding promptly to customers also applies when you answer the phone. Pick up the phone promptly and train your staff to deliver the information that is required by the customer in a friendly and professional manner. If you are unable to give them the information they need immediately, it's essential to assure the customer that you will get back to them as soon as possible with the relevant details. And make sure you do. That customer will be waiting to hear from you and won't want to have to ring you back to find out the information they are waiting for. Leaving people waiting for a return call is an easy way to lose customers and will cost your business dearly in the long run. However, delivering outstanding service has little or no financial cost to the business if you are able to create an excellent service culture within the company that everyone understands and delivers. As Larry Hirst of IBM puts it, 'A customer is delighted when his or her expectations have been exceeded'.

There is no point in having a wonderful service structure if you sell poor products. How can staff feel passionate about selling a product if it is second-rate? If the product is lousy, it doesn't matter how good the customer service is because the customer won't be happy and is unlikely to use the organisation again.

Watch your cash flow

To give your customers the products and services they want, you have to have enough money to be able to buy them in the first place, as well as pay your staff (and yourself too), and settle the bills. Keeping a very close eye on your cash flow is essential for all businesses, but for small companies in particular — in fact, cash-flow crises are the most common reason for business failure in the UK.

'Cash is like the air we breathe. It's vital for survival. You can exist for a long time without profits, but without air you are dead! This is especially so if you have a leak and don't detect it early enough. An undetected leak in your cash flow is as fatal as one in your air supply.' David Henley, business advisor

A positive cash flow is the main ingredient needed for your business to become and (crucially) *to stay* successful. Controlling your costs is key to being able to run a successful business. Make sure you always know how much money you have in the bank and how much money is going out and when.

Your accountant will, of course, be able to advise you on your financial dealings, but ultimately the responsibilty lies with the owner. There is a lot you can do yourself to keep your cash flow healthy and that is why it is essential to do either a weekly or monthly financial report.

Buy stock carefully

Remember, anything that is not sold is dead money, which will have a negative impact on your bottom line. Getting the balance right between buying and selling isn't easy. Retail shops have to be able to afford to stock products that will sell quickly and appeal to their market sector, without overspending and buying so much that they then have to sell the unwanted stock at a reduced rate. Special offers will be popular with your customers, but will knock your profits.

If you are in a seasonal business, it is vitally important that you control your spending and understand your customers' needs clearly. For example, a small dress shop has to be very careful when buying stock for the different seasons. If they end up with an overstock of summer wear that doesn't get sold because of poor weather (always a worry for this market), the profit will be reduced and the owners will have less cash than planned to invest in new winter stock. Get to know what your customers want, and when they want it, so that you can provide it with ease.

Make sure you're paid on time

Retail, leisure and hospitality industries have an advantage in that customers pay at the end of their shopping trip, meal or stay. It's not quite so easy for other businesses, though, and waiting for an invoice to be paid can be excruciating if money is tight and you're due to pay your staff or suppliers at any time now. It's wise to get into some good habits so that you can cut down on some of the stress involved. For example:

- **Invoice promptly.** The sooner you invoice a customer for the work you've done, the sooner you'll be paid.
- **Follow up.** One week after you've sent the invoice, call the customer to make sure they've received it. If there are any problems or questions, you then have a chance to deal with them early.
- **Be strict about your terms of trade.** You're not legally obliged to wait 30 days for payment, although many people think you are. Ask for payment within a fortnight, if possible, but it's best to agree this with your customer early on.
- **Offer a discount for prompt payment if your margins allow.** People love to feel they're getting a bargain, so if (and only if) your margins can take it, offer people, say, 5% off if they pay you within ten working days. Don't make a habit of this, as customers will come to expect it, but it's a good ruse to use if you're trying to speed a tardy payer along.
- **Do a credit check.** Many small businesses fall right into the hands of unscrupulous customers: if they're offered a large order, they're so pleased to get it that they don't think to check out the potential customer first. I urge you to do this if large

sums of money are involved: it's a simple process and not at all expensive. For example, the Companies House website (www. companies-house.gov.uk) enables you to buy a set of accounts for every registered limited company in the UK.

Look at every single cost

If you are dealing with perishable goods such as food and flowers, you have to control your buying rigidly to make sure you have enough to go round but don't buy so much that there is waste. At The Cloud, the head chef has a budget and keeps an eye on food prices as these can vary enormously from day to day. Depending on the seasons and the availability of certain ingredients, my chef has learned to buy competitively priced produce, which enables us to deliver five-star service on a budget. With sensible buying, it is possible to provide excellent meals on a shoestring.

Many restaurants go out of business because they spend far too much money on food, crockery and fancy glasses, as well as being overstaffed. They do not put enough importance on training their staff and therefore cannot give the customers an experience to remember. Expensive plates and glasses don't make food or drink taste any better, and it certainly won't make up for poor service. People don't go back to a restaurant or café time and again because of the crockery: they return when the service is excellent, the food is delicious and there's a warm and friendly atmosphere.

Go easy on advertising

Many small-businesses owners get a bit 'caught in the headlights' with advertising: it's something they think they should do, but aren't sure how to make it happen effectively and without costing a small fortune. If you can afford an advertising budget at all, control it tightly.

One of the biggest and most expensive mistakes I made when I first took over the running of the hotel was to advertise in every magazine, journal and charity programme that rang to sell me space. I just couldn't say no to the pressure that was put on me by the advertising sales personnel, but I soon discovered how little return I was getting for my investment. I eventually realised that if I spent £100 on an advert, I'd have to win at least £1,000 of business before it even began to increase my bottom line. I certainly was not achieving that and I soon learned about other, more successful ways of promoting my business, such as targeted PR (if your budget allows) or even just word of mouth.

The mistake that many people make when advertising their business is that they sell their products and services but forget to sell the benefits of what they're offering. This is exactly what customers want to know: how will buying from you make their lives easier/cheaper/less stressful? They're also looking for a business that will go that extra mile to delight them so the trick is to try and provide your customers with benefits they won't find anywhere else.

For instance, at The Cloud, we're selling relaxation. In our advertising, we focus on being somewhere that allows guests to unwind and relax. We do not have a spa or leisure centre, but we create a warm and friendly atmosphere where customers can feel at home and unwind in a super location. I don't have to invest in millions of pounds in a spa to help my customers relax: I can do that on a shoestring with the right staff and comfortable surroundings but it requires continual attention and hard work to achieve it.

Although an advert has to attract the eye of the reader, you must be careful not to oversell your product and to be sure you can deliver what you are promising to the customer. I always put my customers at the heart of my business and ask myself how would I feel if I read that advert. What experience would I expect to get from it and can I be sure I would get it?

Follow up

Business advisor David Henley believes a very good way of discovering if you have a satisfied customer is to have the 'hit me' call approach. David used to ask his sales staff to make a call to a customer within 24 hours of a sale of a new or used car. They would ask one question: 'Are you entirely satisfied with your purchase?'

In fact, this wasn't another sales call, but what David termed a 'satisfaction call': he wanted to know straight away whether customers were happy with their purchase rather than have them go back to the showroom enraged. The sales staff found that very few customers were unhappy and, even if there was a problem, the fact that the company had called to check and were happy to sort it out gained them a great reputation. David thinks this was a major ingredient in the company's success and far outweighed the cost of the 'hit me' calls. He says he is always surprised at how few follow-up calls he receives from other companies when he's made a major purchase himself.

Set a good standard yourself

There is no better way to build up an excellent reputation of a business than to be reliable, honest and trustworthy and consistent with your products and service. It starts with the quality of service that the staff receive from the management and that they are encouraged to give to each other. Service is not only about looking after your customers, it is also about looking after each other. I believe I am a role model to my staff and I'm aware that they will follow my leadership skills and provide each other with the respect and quality service I expect them to give to the customers. If employees are working for an organisation where the management are full of energy, enthusiasm and have fun, the staff will respond accordingly and deliver the best customer service they can. Be the leader your team deserves and they'll rise to the occasion.

HANDLING CUSTOMER COMPLAINTS

Nobody wants to hear a customer complain, but unfortunately mistakes do happen; it's how you deal with a complaint that really counts. If customers are treated badly, they'll never forget it and that will be the end of your relationship with them. However, if you are able to see a complaint as an opportunity and turn it to your advantage by handling it well, it is possible to win a customer for life.

First things first

Don't panic. Yes, it is disheartening, disappointing and sometimes (if you're caught on a bad day) even infuriating to receive a complaint, but such is life. Brooding about it won't help the situation.

Odd though it may sound, receiving the odd complaint is actually essential to the success of a business: they give you an opportunity to look at how you operate (and why), and then make changes if you need to. There's nothing wrong with making mistakes so long as you don't make too many and you learn from them. It's when you keep making the same mistakes over and over again that there is a problem.

So no more feeling sorry for yourself! It's time to get your act together and make the first important step towards sorting out the issue: show your customers you really care about them.

Silent but dangerous?

Often it's the customers who *don't* complain that do the most damage to your business. They will leave your office, shop or café unhappy, but because they don't tell you this, they deny you the opportunity to rectify their complaint. They will, however, take great pleasure in telling their friends and family about their bad experience; they, in turn, pass it on to other people they know, and so the bad word about your business spreads. Often, it's unfair or very subjective criticism, but as these customers are unlikely to come back and buy from you again, you'll never get to the bottom of it. The aim of any business must be to reduce the complaints it receives and following some of the guidelines in this book will help you to achieve this.

The hospitality industry, in particular, is under a lot of pressure these days to provide 'perfect' services. It is an extremely competitive sector, which means that standards are rising all the time (as establishments try to distinguish themselves from their rivals) and, as a result, customers' expectations are growing at the same rate.

This is, of course, just as it should be: we all want to get value for money and enjoy our precious time off. TV and radio consumer programmes, as well as newspapers, magazines and business publications, have made the public much more aware of their rights. That cuts both ways: it's good to know what you need to do if you feel someone has let you down, but the flipside is that many people seem hell-bent on trying to get something for nothing. A minority wants their money back, come what may, and if they can claim a free holiday in the process, they're thrilled.

Sometimes customers will complain about the most trivial things, but their comments have to be dealt with in the same professional manner to reach a positive result. It would be wonderful to be able to guarantee that everyone had the perfect experience when they bought or used a service or product, but it's never going to happen 100% of the time, no matter how focused you are and how much training your staff have had.

So what can you do to avoid making mistakes in the first place and losing customers as a result?

Make a commitment to great customer care

You're leading by example when you run your own business, so you must take care that you display the same attitude towards customers that you expect your staff to show. Of course, there are people who could try the patience of a saint, but while they're still coming to you for the products and services they want, they're helping to pay the wages. When you recruit new staff, as part of the interview process explain to them exactly what you expect in terms of managing customer relationships and what the positive benefits to the business will be as a result because every business needs a steady stream of customers.

Liz Earle Naturally Active Skincare offers a range of beauty products and treatments made with naturally sourced ingredients. The business is based in the Isle of

Wight, where it has a shop, but most of its sales are done online (www.lizearle.com). The commitment to customer care is evident in every part of its approach, in terms of both before and after sales: purchases arrive simply yet beautifully wrapped, with a note signed by the member of staff who packed the order. The website offers information about the business, its principles and philosophy as well as about the products, of course, by means of factsheets, a chatroom, and a bulletin board. Purchasers are also invited to 'say hello' via a dedicated phone line. As ever, all of these elements may not be appropriate for your business or industry, but some of them most likely will be.

Make sure your staff are trained appropriately

Training is the next key step to success. However small your business, it's vital that every member of the team who is likely to deal with customers knows exactly what their remit is, and how they should handle queries and complaints of any kind. The importance you place on good customer care should be made clear to *everyone*, including delivery men and women, packers and drivers, as well as the person who answers the phone.

The ability to handle complaints effectively should be a key part of that training. You're obviously working to a tight budget, but you don't have to spend a fortune: common sense and practising with some role-play situations will be a great help.

Don't be afraid to empower your staff. You can't be at your office or shop all the time and if they don't know what to do when you're not there, the business will start to come off the rails. Give them some guidance about what the procedures are for managing complaints and make a note of them for future reference: you could put them on your staff intranet, if you have one, or pin them up on a noticeboard. What you want to encourage is a positive attitude that will enable your staff to identify and resolve the problem immediately without always having to refer the complaint to you or another manager or colleague before it can be solved.

It's also a good idea to hold regular meetings with your team so that you can discuss any complaints, how they were handled, and what you can all learn from that. This type of information is extremely valuable, especially to younger or inexperienced staff, as it gives them a frame of reference they can use in case they run into a similar problem themselves. Once you've talked about the issue, take care not to dwell on it for too long, as it can knock confidence and damage your staff's morale and enthusiasm. It's very easy to concentrate so much on the complaints you receive (although, ideally, there won't be too many!) that you can forget all the glowing reports you get from happy and satisfied customers.

Do remember that not every complaint is justified: some will be totally unreasonable or at best very subjective, so you'll need to work together as you learn to recognise customers who make a career out of complaining and those who have a genuine problem that you need to rectify and then learn from. Experience is the best teacher here. Eventually staff will become confident about using their judgement and common sense in these situations and be able to respond positively and creatively to the demands which customers make on them.

When I'm away from my hotel, either on holiday or on a business trip, people often comment on how 'brave' I am to leave the running of my hotel to my staff. My theory is that I know my staff hate having to face a complaint from a customer while I'm not there (or indeed at any time), so they'll do everything in their power to make sure that no one complains while I'm not there. And if such a situation were to arise, I'm confident that they would listen courteously to the customer's concerns and deal with them effectively. They enjoy the responsibility of running the business while I'm away and of knowing that I trust them enough to be able to leave them to deliver the excellent service I expect from them.

Managing complaints in person

Dealing with angry or upset people is always a challenge, however many years' experience you and your staff may have had. Here are some general pointers on managing a complaint:

Take it seriously

Irate customers are not going to calm down if they think the person they're talking to is amused by the fact that their new fridge hasn't been delivered, their lunch was cold, or that an extra nought has been added on to their invoice. If there is space on your premises and enough staff to cover, take the complainant aside into a quiet room where you can speak to them in private.

Listen carefully

'Active listening' is a very useful technique for many types of business situations. What is the complainant *really* saying? As I mentioned earlier you have two ears, two eyes and one mouth – use them in that order and listen carefully before answering.

Defuse tension if possible

Shouting at someone is, of course, unacceptable, but sometimes tempers will fray. If a customer raises their voice to you or one of your staff, you need to calm the situation without resorting to their tactics. One way of doing this is matching their volume at first, but then bringing it down so that the conversation can then continue more appropriately. For example, 'I CAN SEE THAT YOU ARE UPSET by the delay to the delivery, but I'm here to sort this out for you. We can get someone out to you this afternoon if you're available . . .'

Watch your body language

When we feel uncomfortable, we convey our feelings through our body language. To 'protect' ourselves, we fold our arms and cross our legs, sending out defensive signals. Actively try to manage your body language so that it remains open. The complainant will eventually pick up on it, even if only subconsciously!

Don't put it off

Answer the complaint there and then if you can. If that's not possible, aim to resolve it by the end of that working day. Keep in touch with the customer so that he or she is fully informed of what action is being taken.

Give something back

If a customer has genuine grounds for grievance, one way to turn the situation round is by offering them something that shows you want to keep their custom. What you offer will, of course, depend on your products and services, how big the order was, how much the customer has been inconvenienced and how much you want to keep their custom. If it's a question of a product that doesn't work, then you must obviously replace it, but if the complaint is about a different issue, you could consider:

- **waiving delivery charges**
- **extending a guarantee or warranty by a month or two for free**
- **giving a discount on their next purchase**
- **free samples of new products**
- **a complimentary bottle of wine**
- **free tea/ coffee/ sandwich**

None of these will break the bank, but they will show that you are keen to make amends for the problem, you want to keep their custom and show that you care.

Follow up

A few days after the incident has been resolved, contact the customer to check that he or she is happy with the solution. This may not be an attractive option if the customer has been difficult or unpleasant to deal with, but if *you want to keep them* (see below for more on this issue), I advise you to do it.

Managing complaints in writing

If you receive a written complaint, acknowledge it immediately or, if possible, phone the customer. I find you get much better results faster by talking through the problem with the customer and offering a personal apology. It shows that you do care and the customer will usually appreciate the fact that you've tried to remedy the problem quickly.

Many businesses now make it easy for their customers to contact them online, either by e-mail or by filling in a feedback form of some type. If you receive a complaint by e-mail, acknowledge it as if you were writing a formal letter. Be polite, make sure your spelling and grammar are up to scratch (now isn't the time to resort to 'text speak', as many people do in e-mails) but better still offer to phone the customer so that you can resolve the issue promptly in person.

If you can tell that the customer was very angry when they wrote to you, don't be tempted to respond in kind: the last thing you want is a bad-tempered e-mail from you being forwarded on to people all over the country. Never reply to someone when you're annoyed: compose a reply by all means, but then take a short break and come back to it when you're calmer so that you can edit or rephrase it as appropriate.

Managing complaints over the phone

Handling complaints on the phone is probably the trickiest of all to get right and involves skill and tact: you don't have the advantage of being able to pick up on their body language and you don't have the luxury of being able to walk away for a few minutes to collect yourself, as you can do when you're composing an answer to a letter or e-mail. Also, if the customer has been passed around from pillar to post as colleagues try to find the right person for him or her to speak to (not that likely in a small business, but it can happen), you may end up getting the brunt of all their frustration. I had a very unpleasant situation recently. I received a very angry letter of complaint that I thought was justified. I rang the person in question as soon as I received the letter to apologise for the incident and to accept full responsibility, although it was a member of my staff who had sinned! By the end of the conversation we were almost friends and he assured me he would be returning to the hotel after all because of the way the complaint had been handled. Proof that talking to customers directly gets you much better results than just sending a letter of apology.

Here are some useful techniques to help:

- **Try to answer the phone as quickly as possible, within three rings ideally. If an unhappy customer can't get through to talk about their complaint, their mood won't improve.**
- **Keep calm. If the person on the phone is shouting, try the technique mentioned earlier for matching their volume; if that doesn't work, let them shout themselves out before you start talking.**
- **Don't interrupt. Take down details of the complaint so that you can pass them on to others if you can't resolve the issue yourself.**
- **If you can't help immediately, take the complainant's phone number and *ring them back* as soon you can. Don't leave them waiting.**

- Accept responsibility if the complaint is justified. Give the customer some assurance that you understand how they feel and apologise profusely, but certainly don't accept liability if, in your opinion, the complaint is not justified. The customer isn't always right!
- Try to end the conversation on a positive note and thank them for bringing the problem to your attention. Make sure that the issue is followed up (if you're not handling it personally) so that it doesn't come back to haunt you.

Resolving common complaints

Complaints and gripes will vary from industry to industry, but here are some of the most common ones that businesses receive and suggestions on how they can be resolved.

Poor products

Most problems can be avoided if you give customers what they want for the price they want it, when they want it. If you advertise that you offer 'one hour dry-cleaning ... or your money back' and then quibble if people do ask for a refund after you've kept them waiting for longer, your business is never going to be successful. It's better to under-promise and over-deliver, every time. If you're getting repeated complaints about a widget you stock, find a new supplier. Don't just wait for the complaints to go away – if they do, your customers have probably gone with them too.

Slow or unfriendly service

Everyone hates being kept waiting unnecessarily for a product or service. It is infuriating to go into a shop where you're completely ignored by assistants until they've finished their conversation about what happened in *Coronation Street* last night. It gives an extremely poor impression of your business and your staff, and will cost you a lot of money in terms of walk-in business that won't be bothered to wait. Make it clear to your staff that this is unacceptable behaviour. If a member of staff is on the phone taking a work-related call when a customer comes in and there are no colleagues for them to alert, they should either end their phone call and tell the other person they'll call them back, or apologise to the customer and ask him or her to bear with them for just a few minutes.

Showing how keen you or your staff are to help can be a tricky balancing act: people are often put off if they can't get a sales assistant's attention when they have a query, but are sometimes surprised when they're asked if they need any help when they've only been in the shop for 20 seconds. A friendly smile or greeting always goes down well to start with, and then give the customer a few minutes to look round before asking if you can help them find what they're looking for.

Sometimes, keeping a customer waiting is completely unavoidable. I've found that so long as you explain why there has been a delay and also acknowledge their presence with a genuine smile, most people will accept your apology. Again, communication is key: if people feel involved, they'll stay with you without complaining.

Also, try to make up for any delay in another way if you can. At The Cloud, if we keep a customer waiting for a meal in the restaurant because, for instance, there has been a problem in the kitchen, we offer them a complimentary drink with an apology and a brief explanation. Have up-to-date magazines and reading matter in your waiting area so that customers or clients can occupy themselves by reading instead of impatiently watching the clock. The time will pass more quickly if they have something to do.

So many complaints can be avoided by just being alert to your customers' needs. If we notice that a customer is obviously not enjoying their meal, we will investigate promptly and offer to change their meal. Sometimes, there is nothing wrong with the food; it may just not be to their taste. By recognising they are upset, being aware of their mood and actively wanting to improve their experience, you're more likely to win their approval and keep that customer.

Poor attention to detail

Take great care when you're writing to customers or addressing them by name. Everyone likes to hear their name — it makes them feel special and valued — but not if people keep getting it wrong. Always check spellings of names and addresses before sending any correspondence: if you're contacting a prospective customer, you want to make the best possible first impression, so getting the basics right is a good start! If you're not sure, just ask.

Also, listen to your customers when they talk to you. To illustrate, I was widowed in 1991 and occasionally still receive letters addressed to my late husband. A few years ago, I bought some furniture from a company. I chose it, I bought it and I paid for it. I then started receiving mail shots from the company addressed to my late husband. These continued for many years, despite several phone calls from me informing them of their mistake. I'm not sensitive about the situation, but many people would be, and for good reason. Eventually I did get annoyed and made a formal complaint, and I'm pleased to say that I no longer receive letters addressed to Mr Owton. The simple answer is to listen carefully to your customers if you want to please them and to avoid complaints.

Have the courage to let *some* customers go

I have to admit that after 35 years in business I sometimes find it difficult to control my feelings if I think a customer is being totally unreasonable. You have to be able to recognise when a bad customer is not worth keeping, as they can do your business more harm than good with all their gossip and negative attitude. You have to have the courage to just show them the door!

Nobody likes to confront a difficult and unhappy customer and it can be tempting to put it off and file that issue in the 'too difficult to do today' tray. After reading Brian Tracy's book *Eat That Frog! 21 Ways to Stop Procrastinating and Get More Done in Less Time* (2nd ed, Berrett-Koehler, 2007), I have adopted his advice and now aim to do the most difficult tasks of the day as soon as I get to the office. Brian's theory is that there cannot be anything worse than eating a live frog first thing in the morning, so once you have 'done that' i.e. faced the most challenging task of your day first thing, the day can only get better. It really does work for me and I've even pinned a note on my kitchen noticeboard at home to remind me to 'eat the frog'.

That said, not all customers are equal. Clearly you want to aim to grow your customer base by attracting new ones while still retaining (and selling more to) existing, loyal clients. That's the ideal scenario and it's a challenge that never ends. But in reality, some people just aren't worth your spending a lot of time and money on. I don't mean that you need to be rude or dismissive to them, but if you're regularly harangued by someone who isn't making a significant contribution to your bottom line, the next time they threaten to go to a competitor, it may be more cost-effective for you to let them go. Our sister publication, *Boosting sales ... on a Shoestring* by Bob Gorton, covers this topic in more detail.

MY FORMULA FOR SUCCESS

Every business is different and needs to chart its own path through the rigours of everyday life, but there are some basic tenets that are appropriate for all entrepreneurs.

1. Don't give up

It can take a long time for a small business to become established, so don't expect too much too soon. You'll need to be in it for the long haul. It's important to be realistic, but also try to balance that with some goals that keep you stretching and wanting to take the business on to the next level.

2. Focus on your customers

What do they really want? What would make their lives easier? If you're not sure, ask them. Looking after your business is a big personal investment: you're putting a lot of time, effort and energy into it and as a result you will feel very involved. Commitment is great, but remember that *you* are not buying the products and services; other people are. Don't focus on yourself, but on what the market is calling for.

3. Pitch in

Teamwork is important in any business, but some of the most successful entrepreneurs are the ones who roll their sleeves up, get their hands dirty and work occasionally on the shop floor. I started in the hotel business washing up night after night. I then progressed to being a room maid and several years later became a waitress. When my husband died, I cooked all the meals for two years. I have experienced and worked in every section of my hotel and can turn my hand to anything – occasionally I still do if we are short-staffed. I believe you gain the respect and confidence of the staff if they know you understand as much as they do what's involved in the nitty-gritty of making your business work.

4. Surround yourself with good people

On top of your own performance, your business will benefit from having excellent staff and advisors who can help you as you try to grow and develop your services. For example, in terms of your staff, aim to attract star talent and give them star treatment. A company is often judged by the people it keeps! Lead your people as you would like to be led yourself. Value them but also demand excellence and quality service from them at all times.

5. Give something back to your local community

Many small businesses that thrive do so because of their local community. Being sensitive to the needs of others and giving something back to the people who have supported you gives everyone a feel-good factor which is linked to happiness and helps make good relationships even stronger. Helping others less fortunate than yourself and sharing your success with worthy causes is very rewarding and shows that your business cares. I'm not talking about making donations to charity, important though that is, but rather about putting some effort into raising money and having fun in the process. Doing something that everyone can enjoy is often more beneficial to the charity and to your company than just giving a donation.

The ladies of Rylstone WI, now immortalised in the film *Calendar Girls*, are an excellent example of this: when one of their members, Angela Baker, found that her husband John had been diagnosed with non-Hodgkin's lymphoma, the ladies banded together to make their famous calendar which went on to raise over £1 million for leukemia research. Traumatic as this crisis was, Angela did not let it destroy her but took the opportunity to help others in a similar situation and become a stronger person herself.

As Angela puts it: 'Out of a tragedy, we have achieved something so positive. It has certainly been a team effort with friends and family giving us continual support all the way; and it has been an amazing journey! If you have an idea or a dream, go for it; you never know what will happen and your dream could come true – mine did.'

Having a hotel and restaurant gives me the facilities and opportunity to organise charitable events where everyone can enjoy themselves. One of our most popular and rewarding events during the year is when we treat the carers of local people suffering from Alzheimer's to dinner at the hotel. The carers enjoy the opportunity of having just one evening away from their loved ones and are able to relax in each other's company. This is worth more to them than any financial donation we could make.

For many of them, it's the only day of the year they can take a few hours' break from their responsibilities and to see the pleasure it gives them is more rewarding to my staff and me than any financial gains we make. My staff all want to work on those nights as it gives them such pleasure to know they are making people happy and it makes them feel involved. Everyone wants to feel needed and giving something back is an opportunity to show we care for people who care for others.

6. Tell the world!

As I mentioned in Chapter 4, don't be afraid to tell people about what you and your business are doing. Charity events are a good example again: they can give your business free publicity, and being featured in the press will almost certainly draw attention to you and get you some enquiries that will hopefully result in some sales.

Always send a press release to the local newspapers and magazines informing them of your charity events. Journalists do get inundated with these, so to grab their attention, keep it short, entertaining and interesting. If possible, attach a photo of the event as well — anything you can do to make their lives easier for them will be a big plus. Publicity of this type is a win-win situation, as both the charity and your business will see their profits boosted.

I'm often asked to speak at charity events and tell my story. This is another excellent way of bringing your business to the attention of the audience as well as helping the charity to raise much-needed funds. I have acquired numerous new customers from my speaking events and I would encourage anyone who is invited to speak at an event to do so.

The prospect of speaking in public doesn't appeal to everyone, and to be honest I used to be terrified of it myself. (In fact, years ago I couldn't even bring myself to talk to my customers. I used to leave that to my late husband. I'd rather be cleaning the loos. No one could believe how shy I was, because I'd been a dancer, but dancers dance, they don't speak!).

If you have a positive mental attitude you can achieve more than you ever thought possible, so take the initiative, overcome your fear of public speaking, and learn to enjoy it and benefit from it. There's always a chance you will get paid to do it, too! If you never step outside your comfort zone, you will never make progress, because the only limitations we have are those we create ourselves. The biggest challenge is taking that first step towards achieving your goals. Once you've accomplished something you didn't think was possible, it's incredibly empowering.

7. Don't be scared

If you run your own company, you'll be waking up to a new challenge and opportunity every day. At times you may not feel as if you can deal with these, but you can and it will help you to develop as a person. If you have clear goals, a strategy to reach them and the commitment to keep going even when things don't go to plan, the rewards are amazing. Of course you'll have highs and lows as your business gets off the ground, just as you do in every area of life, but mistakes aren't the end of the world so long as you learn from them. If you quit, you will never know what you might have achieved so move on, take the lesson on the chin and don't beat yourself up about it.

8. Keep the ideas flowing

Always be ready to adopt new ideas, both in terms of the products and services you offer and the way you deliver them. Be aware of changes in your marketplace and respond to them as best you can. The Internet has made life much easier in that respect, as you can look at competitors' sites online and see what they're up to, or you can access the relevant industry publications, all from the comfort of your office. Keep your eyes open in your local area. What's new? What's changing?

9. Show your enthusiasm

You are the best advocate your business can have. You know it inside out; you know why it's there and what it's aiming to do.

Make sure that you can explain all of that, in simple terms, to new customers, suppliers and contacts you meet at networking events. Be very clear about your business's purpose so that you can 'sell' it well to others. And don't hide behind the door: be passionate and enthusiastic about everything you do and you'll be able to bring people along with you.

10. Be unique

Aim to give your customers a memorable experience that they won't forget and that will make them want to return. Give them something they won't get from your competitiors. Business in any sector is fiercely competitive these days, so concentrate on the things that are different and that will generate profits. If you chase two rabbits you won't catch either of them. Concentrate on your strengths and not your weaknesses. Make your product the very best you can — remember that customers aren't always looking for the cheapest product, but the one that best suits their needs. Pricing is important, of course, but it doesn't always bring you the loyalty and repeat business that you're after.

Finally, consistency and perseverance are the key to success and I can't impress upon you enough to never give up, because success might be just around the corner. 'By sheer perseverance the snail reached his goal!' Don't let any fears you may have hold you back. Have confidence in yourself and in your business. Confidence is infectious, so let your enthusiasm shine through. As Conrad Hilton neatly summarised it: 'To achieve great things, you must first dream great things.' Because winners never quit and quitters never win. Good luck!

INDEX